The Accountable Juggler

Public Affairs and Policy Administration Series

The Accountable Juggler

The Art of
Leadership in
a Federal
Agency

Beryl A. Radin
University of Baltimore

CQ PRESS

A Division of Congressional Quarterly Inc.
Washington, D.C.

CQ Press
1255 22nd St. N.W., Suite 400
Washington, D.C. 20037

(202) 822-1475; (800) 638-1710

www.cqpress.com

♾ The paper used in this publication meets the minimum requirements of the American National Standard for Information Sciences—Permanence of Paper for Printed Library Materials, ANSI Z39.48-1992.

Printed and bound in the United States of America

05 04 03 02 01   5 4 3 2 1

Cover designed by Karen Doody

Library of Congress Cataloging-in-Publication Data

Radin, Beryl.
    The accountable juggler: the art of leadership in a federal agency / Beryl A. Radin.
        p. cm. —(Public Affairs and Policy Administration series)
    Includes bibliographical references and index.
    ISBN 1-56802-643-9 (alk. paper)
    1. United States. Dept. of Health and Human Services—Management. 2. Public administration—United States. 3. Leadership. I. Title. II Series.

HV91.R333 2002
352.3'0973—dc21   2001007644

Contents

Foreword

There is a scene in the movie *Ben Hur,* in which Ben Hur tries without success to get his four new chariot horses to run swiftly around a track. The bedouin who owns the horses tells him that each horse has its own personality and skills and that they must be harnessed together in a way that allows them to run as a team. That story underscores the essence of successfully managing a large, complex cabinet agency.

Beryl Radin, a distinguished scholar of public administration, has taken on a task almost as difficult as managing and leading the U.S. Department of Health and Human Services (HHS). She has decided to analyze and explain the management and strategic challenges that government leaders face.

Her context is the public administration literature and what it tells us about large, complex public agencies. Her protagonist is a fictitious, newly nominated secretary of HHS. Professor Radin tells this hapless patriot what he needs to know not just to get through his confirmation hearing but also to make a difference during his tenure. Making a difference, according to Professor Radin, requires understanding the different cultures of the various agencies within the department and using accountability and management processes to make the sum larger than the parts.

Not since Professor Roscoe Martin dissected the Tennessee Valley Authority have any scholars steeped themselves in the culture of a large government agency over a substantial period of time and reported their findings with such insight. Professor Radin is an outsider with keen and thoughtful things to say about the work of HHS, the single federal agency that impacts the lives of most Americans. Her discussion of accountability inside and outside the department is a particularly important contribution to the literature.

The most important lesson for a successful leader is flexibility: Standing on principle is not the same as standing in cement. The writers of our Constitution did not create a system in which one side wins all the time. In fact, that was the last thing they wanted. What they wanted was a system in which men and women of good will—although of differing views—could hammer out compromises that would, over time, bring a better life to every citizen. This book tells us how that political and administrative process works.

For any policymaker or student of public administration, this book is the best ever written on a modern cabinet agency. I hope every new cabinet secretary and agency head will read this book after winning confirmation. If they read it before, it might scare them away from public service. If they read it after, it may help them to become stronger, more effective leaders.

Donna E. Shalala
Secretary of Health and Human Services, 1993–2001

Preface

I cannot avoid making explicit what is apparent to anyone who knows me. This book is the work of an HHS/HEW groupie. For many years—longer than I'd care to admit—I have followed the machinations of a department that contained policies and programs that preoccupied me both as a scholar and as a citizen. I began my encounter with what was then called the Department of Health, Education and Welfare when I worked with the U.S. Commission on Civil Rights, concerned about the implementation of civil rights policies within HEW. My doctoral dissertation (and first book) focused on an aspect of that effort—implementation of Title VI of the 1964 Civil Rights Act in the education programs within HEW. I spent a year in the department during the Carter administration, working on a policy document that reviewed the multiple programs within the agency. Coauthoring a book on the creation of the Department of Education gave me still another perspective on what had become the Department of Health and Human Services in 1979. In the years that followed, I continued research on human services policies and the role of the federal government as it attempted to influence the programs that were actually administered by others, particularly state governments.

By the fall of 1995, it seemed that it was again time for me to spend time in HHS. The secretary of the department, Donna Shalala, arranged for me to come into the federal government through the Intergovernmental Personnel Act (legislation that allows faculty members to be hired for short-term appointments). For two years I worked out of the Office of the Assistant Secretary for Management and Budget, first cochairing a departmentwide task force looking at the use and potential of technical assistance efforts within the department and then working with ASMB on the implementation of the Government Performance and Results Act. When I returned to my teaching position in the fall of 1998, for two years I continued to spend a day a week as a consultant with ASMB. In addition, through grants from the PricewaterhouseCoopers Endowment for the Business of Government, I was able to write two monographs on management issues during the Shalala regime in the department.

The combined experiences within the department gave me an appreciation of the challenges faced by a cabinet secretary who attempts to deal with the multiple accountability expectations imposed on him or her by nearly every possible interest group and constituency I could imagine. I felt that much of the literature on cabinet officers and on accountability minimized the cacophony of voices and demands aimed at the secretary. I wanted to present a picture of this job that would give readers a sense of the complexity implicit in the role.

Much of what follows in this volume is not only an attempt to draw on my personal experiences and observations but to place that experience within the academic literature. The book is not an attempt to write a firsthand account of what I saw and did, but it clearly draws on that experience as the basis for analysis. I have tried to use the HHS experience to bring life to a fairly wide range of literatures and theories involving policy and management. It is my hope that the readers of this volume will gain not only an understanding of one department but also with an appreciation of the incredible array of demands that are placed on the cabinet officials who are held responsible for running federal government departments.

My time inside this department reinforced my appreciation of the men and women who make up the federal bureaucracy. For some, the term *bureaucrat* is a pejorative word. For me, it is not. Rather, it describes a group of people who are committed to making the federal government an instrument of caring and respect for all within the society. Although this book highlights the role of the cabinet secretary, much of what is described makes up the world of public servants. They must deal with incredible complexity and with demands coming from nearly every part of American society.

This book therefore is dedicated to those individuals within HHS. I am indebted to their service and to their willingness to share their worlds with me. I am especially indebted to Donna Shalala, the longest-serving secretary of the department.

Several people read drafts of this book. I would like to thank John Callahan, Robert Durant, Judith Feder, Matthew Holden, Don Kettl, and Norma Riccucci as well as the reviewers, Stephen Percy, University of Wisconsin—Milwaukee; Marissa Golden, Bryn Mawr College; Carolyn Thompson, University of North Carolina at Pembroke; Fred Thompson, Willamette University; and Nancy Miller, University of Maryland—Baltimore County. In addition, I have found working with Charisse Kiino of CQ Press a real joy.

Annotated List of Abbreviations and Terms

AARP American Association of Retired Persons. Organization that represents the interest of retirees.

ACF Administration for Children and Families. The unit within HHS responsible for programs for children and families. Includes Head Start, Foster Care and Adoption programs as well as the Low Income Heating and Energy Assistance Program (LIHEAP), Child Abuse and Neglect programs, and the Office of Community Services.

AFDC Aid to Families with Dependent Children. The federal-state program that provided cash assistance to eligible low income families. Replaced by TANF.

AHRQ Agency for Healthcare Research and Quality. The organization that focuses on the quality of health care. Formerly known as AHCPR, the Agency for Health Care Policy and Research.

AoA Administration on Aging. A federal-state program providing services for the elderly.

ASH Assistant Secretary for Health and the Office of the ASH.

ASL Assistant Secretary for Legislation and the Office of the ASL.

ASMB Assistant Secretary for Management and Budget and the Office of the ASMB.

ASPA Assistant Secretary for Public Affairs and the Office of the ASPA.

ASPE Assistant Secretary for Planning and Evaluation and the Office of the ASPE.

ATSDR Agency for Toxic Substances and Disease Registry. Organization linked to CDC that implements environmental health-related laws.

BRB Budget Review Board. The process used internally in HHS to develop the department's budget. Includes the ASMB, the ASPE, and the ASH.

CDC Centers for Disease Control and Prevention. The organization located in Atlanta that focuses on health prevention.

CHIP Child Health Insurance Program. A federal-state program administered by CMS.

CMS Centers for Medicare and Medicaid Services. Formerly HCFA.

DOI Department of the Interior.

ED U.S. Department of Education. Part of HEW until it was made a separate cabinet department in 1979.

EPSDT Early and Periodic Screening, Diagnosis and Treatment. The program within Medicaid that provides health services for low-income children.

Executive Secretariat The unit within the Office of the Secretary that coordinates all activities within the department.

FACA Federal Advisory Committee Act. Establishes requirements for federal agencies to solicit advice from various groups in the society.

FDA Food and Drug Administration. The organization that protects public health by regulating food and drug products. Includes the Hazard Analysis and Critical Control Point program.

FTEs Full-time equivalents. The system for determining personnel levels in agencies.

GAO General Accounting Office. Evaluation and oversight office in the Congress.

GPRA Government Performance and Results Act.

HCFA Health Care Financing Administration. The organization renamed CMS in 2001 that implements the Medicare and Medicaid programs.

Head Start The program within ACF that supports preschool services largely for low-income children.

HEW U.S. Department of Health, Education, and Welfare. Renamed the Department of Health and Human Services when the Department of Education was created in 1979.

HHS U.S. Department of Health and Human Services. Sometimes called DHHS.

HIPAA Health Insurance Portability and Accountability Act.

HRSA Health Resources and Services Administration. The organization that implements programs that seek to promote access to health care services. Includes the Health Centers Program, the National Health Services Corps, the Maternal and Child Health Services Block Grant, the Ryan White HIV/AIDs program, the Organ Transplantation Program, and Emergency Medical Services Program for children.

IHS Indian Health Service. The organization that provides health services to American Indians and Alaska Natives. Governed by the Indian Self-Determination and Education Assistance Act.

Medicaid A joint federal-state program that provides health care for low-income citizens.

Medicare The program administered by HHS that provides health care for retirees.

NGA National Governors' Association.

NIH National Institutes of Health. The unit composed of twenty-five institutes and centers that conduct and support medical research.

NPR National Performance Review. The administrative reform effort during the Clinton administration, led by Vice President Gore.

OEO Office of Economic Opportunity. The War on Poverty agency established in the 1960s. Many of the programs (including Head Start) moved to HHS.

OHDS Office of Human Development Services. The program unit that became ACF.

OIG Office of Inspector General.

OMB Office of Management and Budget. The office within the Executive Office of the President with a number of responsibilities, particularly developing the president's budget.

ONDP Office of National Drug Control Policy. Drug office within the White House.

OS Office of the Secretary. Those units within HHS that report to the secretary and provide advice to that individual.

OSTP Office of Science and Technology Policy. Science office within the White House.

PHS Public Health Service.

PPBS Planning, Program and Budgeting System. Developed in the 1960s to create a more focused budgeting system.

PRWORA Personal Responsibility and Work Opportunity Reconciliation Act. Contains TANF.

Regional Offices Ten offices located throughout the United States headed by regional directors.

SAMHSA Substance Abuse and Mental Health Services Administration. The organization that focuses on mental health and substance abuse services and research. Includes the Center for Mental Health Services, the Center for Substance Abuse Prevention, the Center for Substance Abuse Treatment, and the National Clearinghouse for Alcohol and Drug Information.

SSA Social Security Administration. Part of HHS until it was made an independent agency in 1995.

Staff Offices The units within an organization that provide advice to those with formal authority, that is, those at the top of a hierarchy.

Surgeon General The top medical officer in the federal government.

TANF Temporary Assistance for Needy Families. The federal-state program that replaced AFDC and provides cash assistance to families who meet specific requirements.

UNOS United Network for Organ Sharing. The organization that represents transplant centers.

Y2K Process of ensuring that computer systems were able to respond to the demands of a new millennium.

C h a p t e r

1

Introduction

IT IS THE end of November. A new president has been elected and is in the process of assembling a cabinet. Raymond Wilson, the former California state health director, has just received a phone call from the president-elect, asking him to become the new secretary of the U.S. Department of Health and Human Services (HHS). Wilson is excited about the prospect of assuming that job and without hesitation says yes.

After he puts down the telephone he suddenly realizes that he is not sure what this position entails. Because of his previous job, he does know something about some of the department's health programs, especially those that involve state agencies in the implementation process. But he is not familiar with the rest of the programs of this large, diverse agency. With a bit of panic, he notes that the hearings on his nomination before two Senate committees are scheduled about the same time as the presidential inauguration on January 20. He will have to find ways during the holiday season to prepare for the range of issues that are likely to emerge as the committees test his knowledge of the department.

The department itself has prepared an impressive array of transition materials for a new secretary and the presidential campaign staff put together a group of advisers to brief the new cabinet official. Some of these materials deal with the policy issues that Wilson will inherit; others focus on the issues that were a part of the presidential campaign. Still other materials focus attention on internal management questions that he must confront.

Wilson realizes that he will be held accountable by the general public, the press, the White House, interest groups, and clearly by Congress for all the activities that are a part of the HHS portfolio. Yet he also knows that many of the programs do not provide real authority or direct leverage for the secretary to make changes. Many of the department's programs are not actually implemented by federal officials. Instead, state, local, nonprofit, or private sector agencies implement programs over which the secretary has limited control.

As he plows through the transition materials, he gets a sense of the diversity of those accountability expectations and how difficult it will be to deal with all of them. Clearly, his challenge is to make some sense of this department that has more than 60,000 employees, more than 300 programs, and a budget of more than $400 billion in 2001. Despite the changes that have taken place in the department, where large chunks of the organization have been peeled off (the creation of a separate Department of Education in the 1970s and the decision in the 1990s to make the Social Security Administration a separate entity), it is still very large and complex.

Leading this department will be his greatest challenge yet. Wilson knows that his future success rests on his ability to devise a realistic plan that will allow him to navigate through this organizational world. Over the past week he placed phone calls to former secretaries of the department. Those brief conversations quickly brought a few things home: he must develop a strategy for running the department that not only makes sense for the agency but also meshes with his own personal style and strengths.

His predecessors did not agree on a strategy. Some highlighted the need to make the department highly centralized; others, by contrast, emphasized reliance on the individuals who would be appointed to head the department's numerous bureaus and offices. A few suggested that he simply focus on those issues that are both of interest to him and also a part of the presidential campaign. Others advised him that he needed to be attentive to the entire department; even if he is not an expert in all of its program and policy areas, he will be required to make decisions about issues that are unknown to him.

As he prepares for the confirmation hearings, Wilson decides to make a list of all of the questions that come to his mind. In these questions he tries to capture all the concerns that have surfaced as he works through the materials that have been given to him. He places the questions in four general categories: first, issues dealing with overall strategy; second, questions about the policies and programs within the department; third, political demands on him; and fourth, questions that emerge about the internal management processes within the department.

Questions of Strategy:

- How should the secretary of HHS view the department—as a unified entity or an array of very diffuse programs?
- What is the appropriate image for the secretary to strive for? As he attempts to imprint his role on the department, should he be viewed as a manager, a leader, a political official, or some combination of the above?
- What criteria should the secretary use to assess his success or failure? Should he rely on satisfying political players, focus on achieving the most efficient and least costly approaches, or highlight the substantive performance of the programs within the department?

• How should the secretary think about his level of authority within the U.S. system of shared powers between the three branches of government and between levels of government (federal, state, local)? What does it mean to be viewed as a part of the executive branch?

Questions Dealing with Policy:

• Are there effective ways to sort out the many programs within the department's portfolio?
• Should the secretary emphasize the program design, its policy area, or its possible level of controversy?
• How can the secretary respect the individual cultures, professional expertise, and autonomy of the program units and, at the same time, find a way to deal with the programmatic overlaps among these units?

Questions Dealing with Politics:

• How much attention should the secretary give to the multiple actors involved in the department's operations? How should he sort out the roles of the internal bureaucracy, the interest groups, the Congress, and the White House? How should the secretary think about the public, since so many of the department's programs directly touch citizens?
• Should the secretary attempt to have a direct role in choosing the political appointees that will be named to head the program units? What is the best strategy to ensure that the political team within the department generally shares a set of values and approaches?
• Who can the secretary trust? Should he rely only on the political appointees who will move into the department or can he trust the career public servants who are found within the various programs and offices?

Questions Dealing with Management Processes:

• Is it possible to devise a clear strategy for the department that emphasizes the role of the Office of the Secretary? How should the secretary think about the department's multiple cultures and balance centralized approaches with decentralized efforts?
• How can the secretary develop an approach that is flexible enough to respond to unexpected or crisis issues that are likely to emerge?
• Are there ways that the secretary can identify high-risk programs within the department (that is, programs that are more difficult to implement than others)?
• How should the secretary approach the multiple processes and units that are found within the department to provide information about the legal and fiscal performance of program units?

As he amasses this list of questions, Wilson begins to understand the irony of the advice that he received from his predecessors. The department is so complex that whatever strategy you choose, it contains both opportunities and pitfalls. An elaborate web of constraints is created by the many actors and activities. This means that a secretary of HHS can expect to live in an environment of constant change and emergent demands. Yet his predecessors felt they did make a difference, both within the internal operations of the department and in the way the public viewed policy issues and programs. He is especially taken with an article that former secretary Donna Shalala wrote, providing advice on how to manage in a large, complex organization. In that piece, she offers her ten top lessons for managing a large complex bureaucracy.

1. Know the cultures of your organization.
2. Find ways to ensure that appropriate coordination takes place.
3. Don't overlook the needs and abilities of the career public service.
4. Choose the best and let them do their jobs.
5. Stitch together a loyal team.
6. Stand up and fight for the people who work for you.
7. Set firm goals and priorities and stick with them.
8. Don't forget that politics is always part of policy making.
9. Look for allies where you don't expect to find them.
10. Be flexible, be realistic, and don't expect to win every time.[1]

Wilson also realizes that his predecessors' terms of office varied tremendously in length. Some stayed in the position for less than two years. Others held the job for close to the four years of a presidential administration. Donna Shalala actually was the only HHS secretary to serve for eight years, through the two complete terms of Bill Clinton's administration.

Wilson searches for a metaphor that will characterize his role and approach. He realizes that it is impossible to devise a clear road map. Although he may be able to map the general contours of the roles and responsibilities of the department as well as of those players in its external environment, specific relationships and interests are fluid. If he were to complete the map, some issue or crisis would invariably arise, rendering the document of limited utility.

Finally an image comes to his mind. He remembers attending a performance by the Flying Karamazov Brothers—an avant-garde juggling group that juggles very different elements such as cats, Jell-O, and automobile parts. These performers are unique. They have juxtaposed juggling and music and juggling and theater, and they have developed routines that draw on chaos theory (where the feeder changes randomly while the performers are in constant motion). One of the most popular acts in the group's show calls on the audience to supply any three objects, provided that they are heavier than an ounce, lighter than ten pounds, and no bigger than a breadbox.

Thinking about his future position, Wilson decides that he would be a juggler, too, attempting to keep disparate demands and developments in the air. Can he communicate that to the members of the Senate committee who would decide on his confirmation without sounding as if he were belittling the seriousness of the job?[2]

He has to make sure that he keeps in mind the special role of the department. Closely tied to the diverse fabric of American society, its constituency includes the powerless, the vulnerable, children, the elderly, people with health problems as well as individuals affected by public health and food and drug safety. The comments made by former Health, Education, and Welfare (HEW, the earlier version of HHS) secretary Joseph Califano (who served from 1977 to 1979) strike him as he reflects on his position:

> The New Deal and Great Society programs made the Department of Health, Education and Welfare the place where human hope and human tragedy met in America. For millions of men, women and children, HEW offered the best hope, the only chance of surviving at a minimum level of human dignity. For those seeking help, the Department could be a symbol of past personal failure or an opportunity for a personal future. My job was to make it the latter. . . .[3]

The comments made by Tommy Thompson, secretary of the department during the George W. Bush administration, as he met with HHS employees also seem relevant to Wilson:

> I'm still having a hard time believing that I'm standing here. I'm just a small town boy from Elroy, Wisconsin. . . . I am full of optimism, idealism, and hope—qualities given to me by my hometown and my home state. . . . I am so excited to be here, and while we face incredible challenges, I truly believe that we are at the beginning of a great adventure.[4]

While keeping the image of the juggler in mind, Wilson decides that he would see himself as responding to three types of accountability expectations: policy, politics, and processes. *Policy* focuses on the design of programs and policies; *politics* emphasizes the conflicting accountability demands of interest groups and other partners, Congress, the White House, and experts; *processes* focuses on the internal processes used inside federal agencies to achieve program effectiveness and efficiency. Although they are not as graphic in their differences as the items juggled by the Flying Karamazov Brothers, these three elements are very different from one another. It would be difficult to keep these expectations in the air with precision and skill.

Wilson has learned enough to realize that each of these three elements is likely to pull him in a different direction. What makes sense to the actors who make demands on him in one area may be inappropriate to those involved in another of the elements. He is beginning to recognize the breadth and depth of the various accountability expectations. They go beyond the traditional views about accountability. He must not only satisfy the formal and legal requirements attached to his role but also deal with expectations that have real political consequences.

AN HHS PRIMER

As Wilson prepares for the hearings, a few documents seem to deserve his special attention. Most of them are actually available on the department's Web site.[5] First, he should be clear about the department's historical highlights. Its earliest predecessors date back to the first Marine Hospital, established in 1798, the ancestor of the Public Health Service. The department took form in April 1953 with the creation of a cabinet-level Department of Health, Education, and Welfare. When a separate Department of Education was created in 1979, the department was renamed the Department of Health and Human Services. Although the department has a different name, many of the same issues and problems have continued. (See Appendix 1 for a history of the department, Appendix 2 for the listing and the terms of service of past secretaries, and Appendix 3 for the ten regional offices.)

Wilson also tries to familiarize himself with the organizational structure of the department. The current configuration is composed of eleven program divisions that operate out of HHS headquarters and the ten regional offices distributed across the United States. In addition, an equal number of offices operate out of the Office of the Secretary. See Figure 1.1 for the department's organization chart.

The Department of Health and Human Services is the U.S. government's principal agency for protecting the health of all Americans and providing essential human services, especially for those who are least able to help themselves. It encompasses more than three hundred programs, covering a wide spectrum of activities. Some highlights include:

- Medical and social science research
- Preventing outbreak of infectious disease, including immunization services
- Assuring food and drug safety
- Medicare (health insurance for elderly and disabled Americans) and Medicaid (health insurance for low-income people)
- Financial assistance for low-income families
- Child support enforcement
- Improving maternal and infant health
- Head Start (preschool education and services)
- Preventing child abuse and domestic violence
- Substance abuse treatment and prevention

Figure 1.1 Organization Chart for the U.S. Department of Health and Human Services, circa 2001

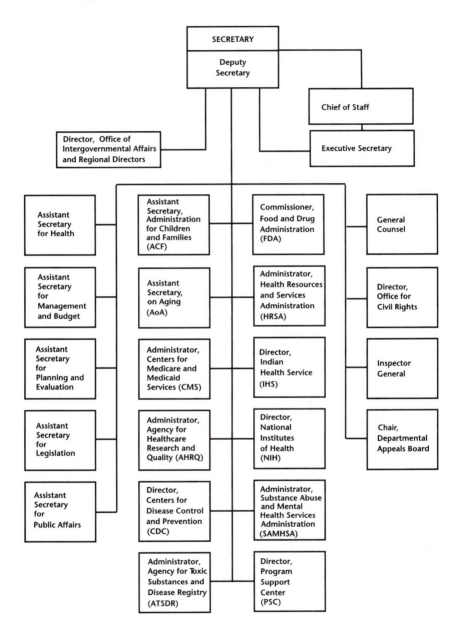

• Services for older Americans, including home-delivered meals
• Comprehensive health services delivery for American Indians and Alaska Natives

HHS is also the largest grant-making agency in the federal government, providing some 60,000 grants per year. Its Medicare program is the nation's largest health insurer, handling more than 900 million claims per year.

The department works closely with state, local, and tribal governments as well, and many HHS-funded services are provided at the local level by state, county, or tribal agencies, or through private sector grantees. In addition to the services they deliver, the HHS programs provide for equitable treatment of beneficiaries nationwide, and they enable the collection of national health and other data.

THIS BOOK

The dilemmas or challenges that face Raymond Wilson are not significantly different in type from those experienced by any new cabinet secretary in the federal government. Although the programs and policies in HHS are more complex and diverse than those found in many other departments, the themes are still the same. Secretaries must balance the range of expectations that are involved in running a federal government cabinet department.

This book is an attempt to provide a sense of this complexity. It focuses on one cabinet department—HHS—and examines the competing pressures that are found within it. Most of the examples that are found in this volume draw from the decade of the 1990s.

The book contains eight chapters. Chapter 2 deals with the literature related to accountability and the issues that are relevant for understanding this department. Although the chapter draws on the classic accountability literature, I have sought to develop a more inclusive framework, moving beyond the formal accountability relationships to include broader policy and political issues. In Chapter 3, I provide the background of HHS, discussing various approaches used by past secretaries, and describing some of the program components within this very complex agency. In doing so, I try to give the reader a sense of the wide span of programs within the department that challenges a department secretary.

Chapter 4 focuses on accountability and the policy lens. I illustrate the variety of policy approaches that have been employed to carry out the federal role and discuss how they differ in regard to the accountability relationships that emanate from them. Chapter 5 deals with the political accountability expectations, including interest groups, Congress, and the White House. It illustrates the political volatility of many of the programs within the department. Chapter 6 highlights internal management processes, particularly organization structure, personnel issues, and the role of the Office of the Secretary. It focuses on the range of administrative approaches that have been employed. Chapter 7 focuses on the various ways the department deals with outside groups and tries to tell its story to the general public. This discussion moves beyond the framework of policy, politics, and processes outlined earlier and offers the reader insight into the difficulties the department has in explaining its activities and decisions to those outside of the agency. Chapter 8 provides concluding observations about accountability as well as about the agency.

Notes

1. Donna E. Shalala, "Are Large Public Organizations Manageable," *Public Administration Review* 58 (July–August 1998): 284–289.

2. Herbert Kaufman used the image of the juggler in his book *The Administrative Behavior of Federal Bureau Chiefs* (Washington, D.C.: Brookings Institution, 1981), 176.

3. Joseph A. Califano Jr., *Governing America: An Insider's Report from the White House and the Cabinet* (New York: Simon and Schuster, 1981), 19.

4. Tommy G. Thompson, introductory remarks to HHS employees, February 2, 2001.

5. The HHS Web site: http://www.hhs.gov.

2

Thinking About Accountability

RAYMOND WILSON is beginning to realize that the legal and fiscal accountability processes that he dealt with as a top official in the California state government did not give him a broad enough perspective to capture what he is hearing and reading as he prepares to become the HHS secretary. As he reviews the questions that have been asked of his predecessors during their confirmation hearings, he sees that these queries reflect a much more extensive perspective than he had experienced in the state. Members of the Senate who sit in on the confirmation hearings can be expected to ask questions about the secretary's role in block grant programs as well as questions about programs that the federal government directly implements. Many of their questions are likely to be extremely technical in nature, focused on detailed programmatic aspects. He knows that these questions often surface as a result of inquiries by interest groups concerned about some of the HHS programs. Rarely do senators ask about the management processes, particularly the kinds of decisions that would be faced by a top executive in a very large organization.

Wilson thinks it will be helpful to have his staff review the literature on accountability to give him a conceptual framework. But he is disappointed in the summary report the staff gave him because they found that much of the accountability literature highlights relatively narrow management, legal, or fiscal expectations. Yet Raymond Wilson thinks it is important to have some knowledge of the existing literature. He really wants to develop a more inclusive framework, one that reflects the reality of the job.

As he begins his analysis of that accountability report he asks himself several questions:

- What criteria should the secretary use to assess his success or failure? Should he rely on satisfying political players, focus on achieving the most efficient and least costly approaches, or highlight the substantive performance of the programs within the department?
- How should the secretary think about his level of authority within the U.S. system of shared powers between the three branches of government and between levels of government (federal, state, local)? What does it mean to be viewed as a part of the executive branch?

THIS CHAPTER provides an overview of the extant accountability literature, reviewing the traditional approach to the topic and highlighting some of the works that have helped to broaden it. Its purpose is to summarize the contemporary demands on accountability that have created or modified a new set of expectations for a cabinet official. In addition, the chapter includes an alternative approach to accountability, using the juggler metaphor, that moves beyond the concept of accountability as control.

ACCOUNTABILITY IN THE U.S. CONTEXT

Accountability has become a commonplace term in the language of government. It is used frequently, but its definition escapes any precision. It is used as a code word to express public frustration, to call for control, and to transmit a range of political agendas. We think about accountability in budget discussions, oversight hearings, press exposés, and political campaigns. Although imprecise, it is still a very important concept. Even a search in the thesaurus indicates a range of possible synonyms. *Liability, answerability, culpability,* and *responsibility* are all words that are associated with the term, and yet each points to a different pathway or direction for someone trying to pin down a more precise definition of *accountability.*

The concept of accountability is fundamental to the construct of the American political system. It raises issues that have received attention from public administration writers for more than sixty years.[1] How much discretion should administrators be given? What is the relationship between administrators and elected officials? One of the major assumptions of a democratic society is that government institutions and processes are answerable to the citizenry for their performance. This notion of expectations for performance is a central component of accountability relationships, and yet performance is often in the eye of the beholder.[2]

Those operating within public agencies face a variety of commitments and obligations that are attached to their role. Some of these commitments are more fundamental and subtle than others, such as to uphold the Constitution, to maintain democracy through openness and access to government decisions, and to seek to discover and achieve the public good. Other commitments are more obvious and explicit, such as to obey and enforce laws, fulfill agency goals, uphold professional standards, provide clientele services efficiently and effectively, achieve programmatic ends of political leadership, satisfy the demands of active supporters, and achieve one's personal goals and career objectives. If lucky, staff and agencies find these multiple commitments mutually reinforcing and compatible. More typically, they find these multiple commitments to be the source of incompatible or conflicting expectations. The job of those who run public agencies is to manage these multiple, diverse, changing, and sometimes conflicting expectations. For example, they may choose to respond, deflect, redefine, or ignore any particular expectation.[3]

The structure of American government, based on the concept of shared powers between separate institutions, establishes the framework or design for any approach to accountability. In that structure, every actor or institution operates in a diffuse system where individuals and institutions are forced to accommodate one another.[4] This Madisonian structure has been described as "a harmonious system of mutual frustration."[5] Each of the institutions has the ability to block the ability of another of the institutions to act, creating shared accountability relationships. These shared relationships involve authority to authorize a budget, to make top-level appointments, and even to decide on how to structure a federal agency.

The complexity that is found in the U.S. system is a direct result of the American political structure. When contrasted with a parliamentary system, where the legislative and executive functions are intertwined, the American system appears to be designed to create roadblocks and obstacles to efficient accountability relationships.

TRADITIONAL APPROACHES
TO ACCOUNTABILITY

Much of the literature that deals with accountability emphasizes its negative and formal aspects. Frequently the term is used to highlight methods that can limit the ability of both political appointees and career public servants in government agencies to exert discretion. At least five different forms are found within the literature: legal constraints, fiscal constraints, political constraints, efficiency norms, and forms that flow from the attempt by those at the top of the hierarchy to control the bureaucracy. Although each of these forms is discussed separately, in practice they constantly interact with one another, reflecting the U.S. system of shared powers. Frequently, the institutions that are charged with overseeing these areas are responsible for more than one of them. For example, the appropriations committees in Congress have formal responsibility for fiscal and budget issues, but these units often use the budget process as a way to communicate political and legal accountability expectations.

Conventional wisdom defines accountability in the public sector as the process of holding individuals or agencies answerable for their performance. The underlying assumption of this perspective is the notion that power and influence flow one way in the relationship, emanating from the controller to the controlled. Individual administrators are not only subject to the power and influence of democratic controls but they also face control mechanisms that are rooted in the organizational and professional contexts within which they work. These contexts provide opportunities for public administrators to behave in ways that comply with organizational and professional standards of performance regardless of whether any democratic controls are invoked. For example, individuals in science and research agencies are often controlled by the norms and expectations of their colleagues in their professions, not by those with formal control over them for budget and authority.

Legal constraints minimize the discretion of public servants, establishing rules and defining sanctions that would operate as a deterrent to those who might act outside the defined confines of their roles. These constraints take the form of laws, standards, rules, regulations, and procedures that frequently define multiple checks on agency action. For example, conflict-of-interest requirements limit the ability of an agency official to take action that even has the appearance of personal gain or a vested interest. This set of constraints has been described as formal legalism and, according to John Burke, "is the denial of discretionary judgment and action on the part of administrative officials. Bureaucrats are not expected to be responsible in an active way; they do not personally heed some call to action."[6] Although the legal constraints flow from the requirements defined by those who are viewed as superiors in the organizational hierarchy or by higher authorities such as legislatures or courts, they do exact a price. Frequently, attention to the rules, regulations, and procedures can compromise efficiency. For instance, checks on managerial authority create multiple decision points, which allow consecutive review and endless opportunities to say no.[7] This situation also acts to dissipate executive authority and initiative.

Fiscal constraints are those requirements that highlight the responsibilities of public servants for the stewardship of public sector dollars. These constraints are felt at various points in the decision making process. The first step is the budget process; based on the proposals developed by departments and agencies, the president proposes a budget to Congress, which then embarks on a fairly convoluted appropriations process. The second step focuses on the execution of the budget. Agencies are required to develop financial management and budget execution policies and standards for financial systems and financial reporting, including audited financial statements, in conformance with government-wide accounting concepts and standards. Each agency oversees the development of accounting systems, financial and accounting policy, cost and other financial management reporting, financial management activities, cash management, credit and debt management, and travel management. Oversight of the expenditure process involves the central agencies (such as the Office of Management and Budget, or OMB) and the U.S. General Accounting Office (GAO), the analytical arm of the Congress.

Political constraints are defined by the various actors who have both authority and influence over those who run government agencies. Francis E. Rourke has argued that there are three centers from which political expectations are found: the outside community, the legislature, and the executive branch itself.[8] Harold Seidman reminds us that programs are packaged in ways that elicit congressional and clientele support.[9] Others have noted that practical politics (that is, the need to elicit support from members of Congress and interest groups) limits the ability of federal agencies to move toward decentralization.[10] Similarly, the executive branch itself has a set of expectations about specific programs and agencies and uses its authority and influence to assert its agenda. Both the executive branch and the legislative branch reflect the agenda of specific interest groups who closely watch the agency's operations. Seemingly technical organizational issues (such as the location of field offices or the organizational location of specific functions) are sometimes viewed by interest groups as symbolic of the status and level of interest in specific programs.

Efficiency expectations are built into many of the traditional approaches to accountability. Carrying forward the heritage of the public administration gurus Frederick Taylor, Woodrow Wilson, and Max Weber, this set of approaches rests on several beliefs. First, there is a cheaper and quicker way to carry out the operations of an agency. Second, administrative tasks can be separated from policy (read political) decisions and players. And third, the adoption of the most efficient way of carrying out responsibilities also ensures fair treatment of all those affected by the agency's work.[11] Others, however, have pointed out that there is an intrinsic conflict between efficiency values and democratic values. David Rosenbloom has noted that congressional involvement in the administrative process reflects this conflict. Legislative-centered public administration, he argues, focuses on open public debate and the representation and participation of interested parties. This rarely results in policies that are the most efficient.[12] The majority principle clearly does not produce the most efficient system.[13]

The focus on hierarchical control of bureaucracy has been the approach to accountability that dominates the public administration field. The Weberian bureaucratic form—a hierarchy in which those at the top provide direction to those below—has been the historical basis for most public organizations. Power is transmitted from those with formal authority (the legislature, the courts, or the chief executive) to the individuals at the top of the organization. This transfer provides legitimacy for those who report through an upward chain of command to the individuals at the top. The image of a machine is the metaphor used to describe the actions of this organization. Individuals at the lower levels of the organization are chosen because of their expertise in achieving a specialized set of tasks.

Many of the federal management reforms that have taken place over the years flow from the assumption that a Weberian bureaucracy is the point of departure for accountability.[14] Control, thus, emanates from the top of the organization. As Frederick Malek, a former Nixon administration adviser, put it, "If the executive branch of government is to be managed effectively, it clearly needs a system for setting priorities, pinpointing responsibility for their achievement, requiring follow-through, and generating enough feedback that programs can be monitored and evaluated from the top."[15] Naturally, this approach reinforces a tendency to build staff capacity at the top of the organization and move toward more centralized activity. This pattern was found throughout the federal government, particularly beginning with President Lyndon Johnson's administration. Offices of secretaries used what are described as staff capacities (such as offices of personnel, budget, legal advisers, planning, public relations) to limit the autonomy of those who were responsible for program management (called line functions).

Others, however, have written about the limitations of the hierarchical control approach. Louis C. Gawthrop notes that studies of the behavior of administrative organizations "place greater importance on the value of the informal, unofficial, and implicit role structure."[16] Martin Landau and Russell Stout Jr. have suggested that to manage is not to control; they point to the reality of organizations that operate in a task environment "that is unregulated, risk-bearing, and problematical. . . . Management is, thus, an experimental process, the point of which is to discover that body of knowledge which eventually permits control."[17]

When one focuses on the details of running public organizations, the strictures that flow from the formal hierarchical characterization seem extremely simplistic. The pyramid of control communicated by the hierarchical approach ignores differences in the kinds of work done by federal organizations as well as the importance of individuals in lower rungs of the hierarchy. Herbert Kaufman's work has focused on the role of second-level officials—those individuals who run bureaus of the federal departments and who are important wielders of power.[18] Mark H. Moore emphasizes the uncertainty that surrounds public organizations and notes that leaders who want to be effective have to be sensitive to differences between specific decision-making systems. He suggests that there are real limits to thinking about management systems as a kind of "production line" rather than a "job shop" where decisions are customized for particular situations.[19] Judith E. Gruber focuses on the reality of democratic control of the bureaucracy and the different types of control that emerge from this reality. Rather than relying on hierarchical control, she emphasizes the importance of procedures that are used to limit the isolation of public bureaucracies, especially efforts that involve various forms of participation with the public.[20]

All these writers provide a picture of federal organizations that looks beyond the hierarchy. Although they differ in their emphases, Kaufman, Moore, and Gruber all challenge an approach to control and accountability that focuses solely on those at the top of organizations.

Still, despite the diversity of approaches that undergird even the traditional concept of accountability, there is a tendency in at least some aspects of the literature to rely on fairly narrow definitions of the term, emphasizing formal and legal perspectives on the topic. Barry Bozeman differentiates accountability from efficiency, performance, and fairness and argues that accountability "is achieved if policies and procedures are implemented in conformance with the purposes prescribed by higher authorities."[21] He does not acknowledge that these "purposes" can also include the values of efficiency, performance, and fairness. Similarly, Joel D. Aberbach and Bert A. Rockman contrast accountability with "responsiveness, adaptability, or flexibility"—values that are also often tied to accountability expectations.[22] These definitions, fairly dramatic contrasts to those mentioned above, accentuate the importance of thinking about the ways that public organizations operate as complex systems, constantly balancing competing values, competing pressures, and competing demands on the time of those who are charged with leading public organizations.

REACHING FOR A BROADER DEFINITION OF ACCOUNTABILITY

Several writers about accountability, however, have attempted to establish a framework for these complex systems, acknowledging that accountability relationships emerge from very different perspectives, roles, and, often, values. These writers move beyond a formal and legalistic approach to accountability. For example, Bernard Rosen emphasizes four requirements in the accountability world:

- Make laws work as intended with a minimum of waste and delay.
- Exercise lawful and sensible administrative discretion.
- Recommend new policies and propose changes in existing policies and programs as needed.
- Enhance citizen confidence in the administrative institutions of government.[23]

Further, Rosen argues that high-level political appointees must develop understanding in many areas. Rosen's list of these areas draws on the issues emphasized by those who are a part of more traditional views of accountability but moves toward a broader perspective on the topic:

1. Agency programs overall and their own specific programs
2. Administration policies as they impinge on relevant agency policies and programs
3. Relations with key people in the three branches of government
4. Organization of the executive branch
5. Relationship of own agency to the president
6. Relationship of own agency to other agencies
7. Relevant government-wide policies (for personnel management, financial management, procurement, etc.)
8. Roles of the central management agencies
9. Relation of federal government to state and local governments on pertinent matters
10. Government's ethical standards
11. Roles of career staff and noncareer appointees in own agency
12. Key people in the organization—their strengths and weaknesses
13. Institutional history[24]

Barbara S. Romzek and Melvin J. Dubnick offer an even broader definition of accountability that moves beyond the formal and legalistic approaches. They point to the multiple expectations involved in accountability relationships, writing that the United States has the pattern of layering one kind of accountability mechanism upon another. These newly designed mechanisms are not substituted for earlier mechanisms; rather, they are added to the mix and result in a pattern of multiple accountability relationships that vary in the source of control (whether it is external or internal to the agency) and the degree of control (whether it involves a high degree of control and close scrutiny or a low degree of control and minimal scrutiny). Romzek and Dubnick emphasize four different types of relationships: legal, political, professional, and bureaucratic. They argue that the American political system, with its fundamental cultural norm of distrust of concentrated government power has made the accountability task of governance extremely complex. The American system of separation of powers means that legitimate performance expectations and accountability relationships emerge from diverse sources wishing to promote very different perspectives, roles, and, often, values.[25]

Adding to this structural diversity is the historical tendency in the United States to layer one kind of accountability mechanism upon another.[26] As one kind of accountability problem or scandal emerges, mechanisms are designed to attempt to ensure that such an event can never recur. The pattern has resulted in

Table 2.1 Types of Accountability Mechanisms

Degree of control	Source of control	
	Internal	*External*
High	Hierarchial	Legal
Low	Professional	Political

four different types of accountability relationships: hierarchical, legal, professional, and political. See Table 2.1.

Hierarchical accountability: Hierarchical accountability relationships are defined internally and exhibit a high degree of control. They are manifested in organizational roles, supervisory relationships, rules, standard operating procedures, and close, detailed scrutiny of employee or agency performance. The relationships are based on an expectation of obedience to organizational directives. This type of accountability is found in the traditional approaches to the subject. It assumes that the pyramid that formally describes organizations actually results in controlling relationships.

Legal accountability: Legal accountability relationships derive from external sources that exercise a high degree of control and scrutiny. They are manifested in oversight and monitoring activities. Some actor (individual or organization) external to the office or agency has an independent basis for scrutinizing performance, such as an auditor, a legislative oversight hearing, or a court review of administrative practices.

In both legal and hierarchical accountability relationships, there is little choice about whether to respond to the relevant expectations. The high degree of control and scrutiny leaves little room for discretion; in contrast, both professional and political accountability relationships allow a high degree of discretion as to how to respond to expectations for performance. The scrutiny that does occur is less frequent and less detailed.

Professional accountability: Professional accountability relationships derive from within the organization and involve low degrees of control but high degrees of discretion by the individual or agency answering for performance. These relationships defer to the expertise of the administrator (or agency), who is expected to exercise discretion in a manner consistent with the norms of his or her profession. This control emanates from within the organization as internalized professional norms and standards. Rarely do these expectations result in formal accountability requirements. Rather, they are found in informal relationships within many organizations.

Political accountability: Political accountability relationships derive from external sources and involve low degrees of direct control. They are manifested in a high degree of discretion for the individual or agency to choose whether or not to respond to the expectations of some key external stakeholder and to face the consequences of that decision. The relationship is based on an expectation of responsiveness to these stakeholders. Some of the stakeholders (for example, those in legislative positions) hold formal positions of authority. Many, however, have influence within the broader political system. For example, interest groups do not have formal authority yet they often communicate their accountability expectations to agency officials.

Romzek and Dubnick note that in the American system of governance, any one agency or individual usually operates under one or two types of accountability mechanisms on a daily basis while the other types lie underutilized or dormant. These dormant types typically are triggered in instances of agency crisis or scandal. Under such circumstances, all four types of accountability relationships can be invoked simultaneously and staffers and agencies can find themselves being asked to answer for their performance under multiple standards of accountability.

Although various forms of accountability are found in all organizations, Rosen and Romzek and Dubnick highlight the special characteristics of accountability that are present in public organizations. Their approaches look to relationships that flow from the relationships outlined in the U.S. Constitution and other laws that define public bureaucracies. As a result, they do not attempt to draw parallels to various approaches to accountability that might be drawn from the private sector. To that extent, they echo an argument made by former labor secretary Robert B. Reich: "Democracy is noisy, intrusive, frustrating, time consuming, unpredictable, and chaotic. But it is also the best system of government yet devised for ensuring that government is accountable to its citizens."[27]

Those who find themselves in positions of responsibility in the public sector (such as those in cabinet positions) often characterize their accountability responsibilities as a form of leadership. Although not focusing directly on accountability, the work of Jameson Doig and Erwin Hargrove on entrepreneurial leaders helps one think about the relationship between leadership and accountability. Doig and Hargrove have identified six dimensions that make individual leaders effective:

1. Identify new missions and programs for their organizations.
2. Develop and nourish external constituencies.
3. Create internal constituencies.
4. Enhance the organization's technical expertise.
5. Motivate and provide training for members of the organization.
6. Systematically scan organizational routes, and points of internal and external pressure, in order to identify areas of vulnerability.[28]

Focusing on leadership helps to move the discussion of accountability from a narrow, mechanistic approach to one that emphasizes strategies and tactics.

CONTEMPORARY DEMANDS ON ACCOUNTABILITY

The writings of Rosen, Romzek and Dubnick, and Doig and Hargrove help us to develop a more inclusive definition of accountability. However, a contemporary leader in a public organization has to deal with an even more complex world than that faced by his or her predecessors twenty or thirty years ago. The public sector world that was assumed by most of the writers cited above is now much different from what it was in the past. Whether one focuses on the broad parameters of the reinvention movement, performance measurement, devolution of responsibility through contracting out, or movement of responsibility from one level of government to another, it is clear that changes have occurred throughout the public sector in the United States. Indeed, the shifts observed in the United States seem to be part of an international phenomenon, called the New Public Management.[29] As Edward P. Weber has noted, these changes have emphasized different combinations and types of sectors. He suggests that each one of the different conceptualizations of the role of the bureaucracy in a democracy "emphasizes different institutions and locates the ultimate authority for accountability in differing combinations and types of sectors (public, private, intermediary), processes, decision rules, knowledge, and values."[30]

Although changes have occurred throughout the society, the changes in the federal bureaucracy are perhaps the most dramatic. The federal bureaucracy today is very different from the organizational structure that operated in the past fifty years. These shifts, which have occurred throughout the federal government, not simply in the HHS world, include:

- An appreciation of the close interrelationship between management decisions and policy outcomes
- Increased public expectations about performance of government agencies
- A movement away from the norm of centralized organizations to various forms of decentralized systems
- A movement away from the "one best way" attitude toward management decisions and an appreciation of the use of multiple strategies that are appropriate for different agencies
- Diminution of the role of the federal agency as deliverer of services
- An increase in the devolution of authority to states and localities
- A dramatic increase in the contracting out of services outside the public sector
- An increase in the level of controversy surrounding many issues, particularly involving domestic programs

- A shift in the boundaries of issues and growing expectations of interagency and crosscutting efforts
- Changes in technology and communication mechanisms.

The combination of these issues has changed not only the internal dynamics of federal agencies but also the external expectations about the way they operate. Thus it is important to acknowledge that the combination of internal and external shifts has created a new set of accountability expectations for federal departments. As Romzek and Dubnick have suggested, these expectations are heaped on top of existing demands of the past. Whether or not the approaches, models, and theories that have been inherited make sense within this changed environment, the expectations that are attached to them continue to place demands on officials. These expectations can lead to a situation in which officials feel trapped in a maze.

One of the most common problems related to the piling on of expectations stems from an over-reliance on hierarchical accountability. If a top official believes that the staff who appear on an organization chart are responsible only to him or her, that individual is likely to ignore the relationship between politics and policy making. Although the acknowledgment that politics and policy making interpenetrate public administration is not new, it has become more obvious in the contemporary situation. Many decisions that had been viewed as in the technical purview of officials have now been subject to demands from outside forces. Separation of politics and administration—discredited in the academic literature for some years—seems to be even more inappropriate as the society enters the new millennium, because both the public and political actors challenge the exertion of discretion by managers.[31] An observation made by Paul H. Appleby more than fifty years ago is worth accentuating:

> Arguments about the application of policy are essentially arguments about policy. Actual operations are conducted in a field across which mighty forces contend; the forces constitute policy situations. Administration is constantly engaged in a reconciliation of these forces, while leadership exerts itself in that process of reconciliation and through the interstices of the interlacing power lines that cut across the field.[32]

The public today is more conscious than ever before of the reality of constant change. The traditional ways of thinking about accountability tend to downplay the shifts that take place in a society as diverse and vibrant as that of the United States. The literature has not captured the turbulence associated with America's ever-changing environment. As Garry Wills has noted, the U.S. system of government and the values that undergird it uphold very different directions, moving back and forth between liberal and conservative positions. When government is opposed, we believe "that government, as a necessary evil, should be kept at a minimum; and that legitimate social activity should be provincial, amateur, authentic, spontaneous, candid, homogeneous, traditional, popular, organic, rights-oriented, religious, voluntary, participatory, and rotational." At the same time, we believe "that government is sometimes a positive good, and that it should be cosmopolitan, expert, authoritative, efficient, confidential, articulated in its parts, progressive, elite, mechanical, duties-oriented, secular, regulatory, and delegative."[33]

Given these conflicting values, the American political system—with its fundamental cultural norm of distrust of concentrated governmental power—has always made the accountability task of governance extremely complex. But recent skepticism about government has increased this sense of distrust. Martha Derthick's study of the Social Security Administration points to the consequences for management of federal agencies of both the multiple values within the society and the results of shared power. She writes:

> It is at the oversight stage that an agency feels the full impact of the separation of powers. Under the system of separated powers, although the agency has several sources of command, it has no reliable source of protection when things go wrong. . . . Because no single institution is preeminently in charge of agency conduct, none must accept responsibility when it falters. In distress, it is isolated, a naked object of blame.[34]

Further, she notes that many changes that have occurred in the relationship between the agency and its environment have complicated the administrative task. These include federalism, the propensity of the president to sponsor policy initiatives, as well as interbranch and interparty differences.[35]

Many contemporary writers about bureaucracy have sought ways to avoid the problems that Derthick and others have described. David Osborne and Ted Gaebler's call for entrepreneurial government as a way of assuring a new accountability system rests on the development of performance measures and information about the results of government spending.[36] Robert D. Behn's volume also links an improvement in what he calls democratic accountability to the development of new modes of performance assessment.[37] But these writers tend to ignore or at least underplay both the conflicting values in the American society described by Wills and the consequences of living with an institutional system of shared powers and divided government.[38] Neither seems to confront what Barry Bozeman observed—that accountability is costly.[39]

THINKING ABOUT ACCOUNTABILITY AS A JUGGLING PROCESS

Accountability moves far beyond formal processes associated with control. It reaches into the attributes of the American political system where values and pressures are at play. Thus accountability in the federal government in the twenty-first century requires public sector leaders who are able to juggle multiple pressures, actors, and processes. By examining three different types of expectations that face a cabinet secretary—*policy, politics,* and *processes*—we can try to capture the informal as well as the formal demands and expectations that emerge from the American political system.

The policy expectations: The traditional approaches to accountability have tended to ignore the policy dimension of the process. But policy dimensions are important because accountability relationships are defined within the contours of program design and the traditions of different policy cultures. Accountability for a block grant program that provides funds to third parties (often state or local government) is quite different from accountability for a program that provides services directly to the public through federal staff. Similarly, the historical relationships of some policy areas exhibit a high degree of agreement on program goals, objectives, and implementation technologies whereas those of other policy areas are characterized by contentiousness and conflict.

The political expectations: This set of expectations flows from the complex set of relationships that are attached to the U.S. decision-making system as well as other aspects of fragmented authority. Shared powers have created pressures for all administrative agencies, but those between the White House and Congress are particularly difficult because both institutions deal with top-level appointments, the budget, program authority, and relationships with those who are concerned about the business of governance. Political expectations come from the White House, from the multiple committees and subcommittees of Congress that are involved in appropriations and the authorizing process, and—of no small account—from interest groups and others who may be involved in the implementation of programs. These expectations vary from program to program, reflecting the relationships between the various players. In many instances, the expectations also include conflicting demands.

Management and internal process expectations: Managing the internal operations of a federal department involves many classic management issues. It relates to leadership style, questions of centralization and decentralization (in regard to program autonomy as well as the role of regional offices), the role of the Office of the Secretary, development of the budget, legislation and regulations, and dealing with other federal agencies in areas in which program operations and goals overlap. It also involves relationships between career staff and political appointees.

These three areas define the world of a cabinet secretary in the twenty-first century. They create pressures and demands that push and pull an individual in multiple directions. They provide the framework within which to anticipate the sources—if not the substance—of such pressures and demands. These areas help a cabinet official define the space in which he or she operates. The definition of these three forces allows such an individual to think about accountability expectations in a way that defines how he or she behaves in a day-to-day fashion. A new cabinet secretary is required to find a way to scope the landscape in which he or she operates, always keeping in motion. These three forces define the world of the accountable juggler.

Several decades ago Herbert Kaufman characterized the demands on top federal officials as a process requiring "a juggler's disposition." He wrote:

> Some people do not function well when they have to shift their minds back and forth among different, widely disparate matters in rapid-fire order. They are at their best if they can stay within a single, coherent set of tasks until they complete it and then move to another.
>
> There are some, on the other hand, for whom dealing with many things simultaneously is more congenial. They find it stimulating and exciting to keep many balls in the air at once. Doing one thing at a time bores them. . . . They may go from an issue of national policy to the problem of a single employee, from an intense struggle over substance to a light-hearted ceremony, from giving testimony at a legislative hearing to receiving a presentation by an interest group or staff. The most constant characteristics of their work are its diversity, fragmentation, and velocity.[40]

Although many of the issues involving accountability that have emerged in recent years have been discussed in general terms, there is a lack of literature that focuses on them in the context of specific agencies and specific programs. Few works have captured the ways that agencies and their leaders have struggled with these changes. Although this volume deals with the generic changes and issues that have emerged over the past decade, I attempt to discuss these topics in a way that will help people appreciate the diverse and difficult tasks that have been given to the federal government by focusing on a very large federal department—the Department of Health and Human Services. Thus the book is designed to show how shifts in the classic concern about accountability results in substantive program outcomes: for example, who receives benefits, what kinds of programs will emerge from the department.

Given the complexity of HHS or any federal agency for that matter, there is not a single accountability approach that fits all the situations that are found within a department's portfolio. Instead of attempting to identify a "one size fits all" approach to accountability, I seek to describe the alternative approaches to accountability that must be balanced by an HHS secretary, reflecting the differences in policy or program design, political realities, and demands on administrative processes.

Notes

1. See, for example, Herman Finer, "Administrative Responsibility and Democratic Government," *Public Administration Review* 1 (1941): 335–350, and Carl J. Friedrich, "Public Policy and the Nature of Administrative Responsibility," in *Public Policy,* ed. C. J. Friedrich and E. S. Mason (Cambridge: Harvard University Press, 1940).

2. See Melvin J. Dubnick and Barbara S. Romzek, *American Public Administration: Politics and the Management of Expectations* (New York: Macmillan, 1991); also Melvin J. Dubnick and Barbara S. Romzek, "Accountability and the Centrality of Expectations in American Public Administration," *Research in Public Administration* 2 (1993): 37–78.

3. See discussion in Beryl A. Radin and Barbara S. Romzek, "Accountability Expectations in an Intergovernmental Arena: The National Rural Development Partnership," *Publius* 26, (1996).

4. Joel D. Aberbach, *Keeping a Watchful Eye: The Politics of Congressional Oversight* (Washington, D.C.: Brookings Institution, 1990), 3.

5. James MacGregor Burns, speaking of Richard Hofstadter, quoted in ibid.

6. John Burke, *Bureaucratic Responsibility* (Baltimore: Johns Hopkins University Press, 1986), 10.

7. Martin A. Levin and Mary Bryna Sanger, *Making Government Work* (San Francisco: Jossey-Bass, 1994), 70–71.

8. Francis E. Rourke, *Bureaucracy, Politics, and Public Policy* (Boston: Little, Brown, 1969), 12.

9. Harold Seidman, *Politics, Position, and Power: The Dynamics of Federal Organization,* 2d ed. (New York: Oxford University Press, 1977), 34.

10. Bruce L. R. Smith, "Major Trends in American Public Administration," in Bruce L. R. Smith and James D. Carroll, *Improving the Accountability and Performance of Government* (Washington, D.C.: Brookings Institution, 1982), 6.

11. These issues are discussed in Robert D. Behn, *Rethinking Democratic Accountability* (Washington, D.C.: Brookings Institution Press, 2001), chap. 3.

12. David H. Rosenbloom, *Building a Legislative-Centered Public Administration: Congress and the Administrative State, 1946–1999* (Tuscaloosa: University of Alabama Press, 2000), 147.

13. See discussion in James W. Fesler and Donald F. Kettl, *The Politics of the Administrative Process* (Chatham, N.J.: Chatham House, 1991), 318.

14. See, for example, the scientific management tide found in Paul C. Light, *The Tides of Reform: Making Government Work, 1945–1995* (New Haven, Conn.: Yale University Press, 1997), 21.

15. Frederic V. Malek, *Washington's Hidden Tragedy: The Failure to Make Government Work* (New York: Free Press, 1978), 148.

16. Louis C. Gawthrop, *Bureaucratic Behavior in the Executive Branch: An Analysis of Organizational Change* (New York: Free Press, 1969), 32.

17. Martin Landau and Russell Stout Jr., "To Manage Is Not to Control: Or the Folly of Type II Errors," *Public Administration Review* 39 (March–April 1979): 149.

18. Herbert Kaufman, *The Administrative Behavior of Federal Bureau Chiefs* (Washington, D.C.: Brookings Institution, 1981).

19. Mark H. Moore, *Creating Public Value: Strategic Management in Government* (Cambridge: Harvard University Press, 1995), 170.

20. Judith E. Gruber, *Controlling Bureaucracies: Dilemmas in Democratic Governance* (Berkeley: University of California Press, 1987), 19.

21. Barry Bozeman, *Bureaucracy and Red Tape* (Upper Saddle River, N.J.: Prentice Hall, 2000), 165.

22. Joel D. Aberbach and Bert A. Rockman, *In the Web of Politics: Three Decades of the U.S. Federal Executive* (Washington, D.C.: Brookings Institution Press, 2000), 15.

23. See Bernard Rosen, *Holding Government Bureaucracies Accountable,* 3d ed. (Westport, Conn.: Praeger, 1998), 4.

24. Ibid., 23.

25. Barbara S. Romzek and Melvin J. Dubnick, "Accountability in the Public Sector: Lessons from the Challenger Tragedy," *Public Administration Review* 47 (May–June, 1987): 227–238.

26. This is similar to the pattern of multiple approaches to management reform described in Light, *The Tides of Reform.*

27. Robert B. Reich, *Public Management in a Democratic Society* (Englewood Cliffs, N.J.: Prentice Hall, 1990), 4.

28. Jameson W. Doig and Erwin C. Hargrove, "'Leadership' and Political Analysis," in *Leadership and Innovation: Entrepreneurs in Government,* ed. Jameson W. Doig and Erwin C. Hargrove (Baltimore: Johns Hopkins University Press, 1990), 7–8.

29. See Michael Barzelay, *The New Public Management: Improving Research and Policy Dialogue* (Berkeley: University of California Press, 2001).

30. Edward P. Weber, "The Question of Accountability in Historical Perspective," *Administration and Society* 31 (September 1999): 453.

31. Laurence E. Lynn Jr. has argued that traditional public administration was richer and more focused on the dilemmas of democratic administration than some have suggested. See Laurence E. Lynn Jr., "The Myth of the Bureaucratic Paradigm," *Public Administration Review* 61 (March–April 2001): 144–160.

32. Paul H. Appleby, *Policy and Administration* (University: University of Alabama Press, 1949), quoted in John J. Kirlin, "The Big Questions of Public Administration in a Democracy," *Public Administration Review* 56 (September–October, 1996): 417.

33. Garry Wills, *A Necessary Evil: A History of American Distrust of Government* (New York: Simon and Schuster, 1999), 17–18.

34. Martha Derthick, *Agency Under Stress: The Social Security Administration in American Government* (Washington, D.C.: Brookings Institution, 1990), 171.

35. Ibid., 200–201.

36. David Osborne and Ted Gaebler, *Reinventing Government* (Reading, Mass.: Addison Wesley, 1992), 136–137.

37. Robert D. Behn, *Rethinking Democratic Accountability* (Washington, D.C.: Brookings Institution, 2001).

38. See Radin and Romzek, "Accountability Expectations in an Intergovernmental Arena."

39. Bozeman, *Bureaucracy and Red Tape,* 3.

40. Kaufman, *The Administrative Behavior of Federal Bureau Chiefs,* 176–177.

3

Can Anybody Manage
This Organization?
The HHS Case

AS THE DATE for his confirmation hearings comes closer, Raymond Wilson is trying to find ways to familiarize himself with the department. He finds it difficult to keep the various pieces of HHS in his head at once. The idea of actually juggling those elements is overwhelming. Because of his experience in the health field, he has some knowledge of many of the health programs within the department. But he knows that his responsibility as secretary of the department goes far beyond those programs. The three hundred or so programs within the department encompass many different policy areas. And to make matters even more complex, he learns that the names of some of the program units have changed just in the past few months. One could easily characterize the programs in the department as a moving target.

Wilson decides that he needs to prepare for this hearing much as he would prepare for an examination. He puts the names of all the program units and program components on index cards and asks members of his family to quiz him on them. He tries to sort the more than three hundred cards into categories but sometimes can't decide in what category to place a single card. Based on his review of past confirmation hearings, he is likely to be asked about specific programs; hence he needs to have both depth and breadth in his knowledge, learning about the details of programs as well as about the diversity of initiatives.

Wilson knows that HHS is not one of the older departments in the cabinet. The State Department, Defense Department, and Justice Department go back almost to the founding of the country. The predecessor to HHS—the Department of Health, Education, and Welfare—was not created until 1953, but HHS is much more diverse than some of the older units. To make it even more complicated, programs have moved in and out of HEW/HHS over the years. It is a real challenge for Wilson to become familiar with the breadth of this organization.

He reviews some of the questions that he asked himself early in his job preparation:

• How should the secretary of HHS view the department—as a unified entity or an array of very diffuse programs?
• What is the appropriate image for the secretary to strive for? As he attempts to imprint his role on the department, should he be viewed as a manager, a leader, a political official, or some combination of the above?

THIS CHAPTER attempts to do two things that are relevant to Raymond Wilson's preparation for his hearing. First, it looks at the strategic decisions that have confronted department secretaries in the past. And second, it seeks to focus on some of the programs and program units found within the HHS portfolio that seem likely to require his attention. Like the Flying Karamazov Brothers who respond to items given them by the audience, his juggling task is fluid and often unpredictable.

HHS/HEW HISTORY: STRATEGIC CHOICES

In 1974 Rufus E. Miles Jr., a former top official in the U.S. Department of Health, Education, and Welfare, published a volume titled *The Department of H.E.W.* Dedicated "To the Unsung Career Employees of HEW," this book is the only attempt to focus on the role of this cabinet department in light of changes in the American society. The preface to Miles's book emphasized two themes: first, to catalog the growth of the department "from a loose conglomeration of modest-sized bureaus to the largest department in the world—in expenditure terms—in a mere two decades" and second, "to put the dynamics of HEW into the context of the corresponding dynamics of the larger society." [1]

In that book, Miles argued that HEW is "the foremost institutional expression of five social revolutions that have, within a single generation, completely altered the relationship between U.S. citizens and their national government." The five social revolutions were the New Deal, the education revolution, the civil rights revolution, the health revolution, and the consumer rights revolution. Miles noted that when the department was created in 1953, few of its architects would have anticipated its enormous growth. By 1973 the department included two hundred programs, administered through thirteen operating agencies—three of which were located within the Office of the Secretary—and ten regional offices. Six health agencies were grouped under the Public Health Service, and two education agencies were under the Education Division.[2] See Figure 3.1 for the organization chart circa 1973.

At the time Miles wrote his book, then-president Richard M. Nixon proposed to reorganize the department to give it even broader responsibilities, moving various elements from the Department of Labor, the Department of Agriculture, and other programs to a projected Department of Human Resources. This was part of a general strategy within the Nixon administration to create fewer cabinet departments and centralize authority. According to Miles, "The effort to create a super Department of Human Resources represents an intuitive compromise between the extreme of a single domestic department and the asserted need to interrelate, within a few very large departments, most of the numerous and intertwined federal activities concerned with promoting the general public."[3]

Miles was skeptical about the creation of such a mega-department and did not believe that focusing on the organizational structure was the answer to what he called the "swirling currents of revolutionary change" that surrounded the department at the time. He concluded his study by reminding the reader that all the programs in the department were not under its control: [4]

> But with the conspicuous exception of Social Security, most [of the programs] are under the control of states, local communities, and institutions. The problem of determining whether each such program is accomplishing anything, and if so, what and how much, is enormously more complex than evaluating the performance of a C-5A military transport plane. Evaluation of relative success or failure of HEW's numerous grant-in-aid programs will require almost a quantum jump in the sophistication of social science research and evaluation techniques. If we wish to preserve diversity and avoid enforced uniformity, we may not even be able to establish quantifiable national objectives against which all communities and institutions must measure their progress, as the operations research analysts would have us do.[5]

Miles's skepticism about the creation of a mega-department collided with the prevailing views of Nixon's political advisers as well as many leaders in the public administration community. Both groups believed that reorganizing the government structure in order to place related programs in one organization would go a

Figure 3.1 Organization Chart of the Department of Health, Education, and Welfare, circa 1973

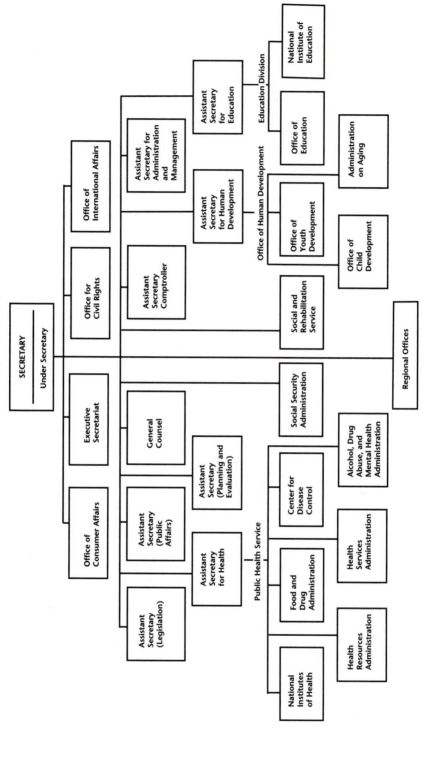

long way toward improving the efficiency of government operations and the delivery of services to the American people.[6] Fragmentation, they believed, led to inefficient, costly, and nonresponsive service delivery. However, these views were not shared by most members of Congress, given their strong symbiotic relationships with interest groups and program bureaucracies. Because of the legislative branch's fragmented structure, members of Congress tend to be skeptical of proposals that concentrate power, programs, or funds into a single department.[7]

AN INTERNAL CENTRALIZATION STRATEGY

When the federal government's involvement in social programs increased dramatically in the 1960s and the structural reorganization schemes failed to develop congressional support, new attention was focused on HEW's internal operations. To that point, the department—like the Department of Defense—had operated much like a collection of separate entities. Indeed, some even described the department as a feudal system in which power and authority were found in the separate components and the head of the "kingdom" operated more like a titular leader rather than one with actual control.[8]

By the mid-1960s, however, the Office of the Secretary had emerged as a power within the department. The span of activity grew wider as the federal government became a more important force in the society. According to the General Accounting Office, the "Secretary's responsibilities have evolved from increasing the Department's administrative efficiency to leading the national response to health and welfare problems."[9] Building on two processes—controlling the budget process and determining departmental positions on legislation—the Office of the Secretary grew and attempted to bring together the separate forces within the program components and reach for a common set of policy goals within the department. For the most part, the role of the staff assistant secretaries in the department was to help the secretary knit together related functions in the operating agencies.

Former HEW secretary Elliot Richardson, secretary from 1970 to 1973, conceptualized the management role of a federal department along three dimensions:

- Developing and refining policies and programs through planning, evaluation, and policy making
- Managing day-to-day, routine activities, such as issuing Social Security checks
- Responding to emerging situations and crises, such as public health epidemics and product tampering incidents[10]

Some of these arguments resurfaced during the Carter administration in the late 1970s. During his campaign Jimmy Carter promised to create a separate cabinet-level Department of Education, thus ensuring the support of powerful education constituency groups. Ironically, Carter's personal approach to organizational structure in Georgia centered on consolidation of government units with overlapping functions and reduction of the number of department and agency heads who reported to him. Although he continued this approach in other program areas, the campaign promise to split HEW and create a separate Education Department finally prevailed. However, during the process of formulating alternative approaches to the reorganization, the proposal to create a mega-department was again considered.[11]

At about the same time the Carter White House considered this umbrella agency, the HEW secretary at the time, Joseph Califano, undertook a fairly major internal reorganization of the department, seeking to imprint his style and agenda on the agency. He described it as "the largest reorganization in HEW's twenty-five-year history, moving around $52 billion in federal programs and more than 50,000 employees." Califano created the Health Care Financing Administration (combining Medicare and Medicaid), formed an agency made up of cash payments in the Social Security Administration, created an Office of Human Development Services, and reorganized the Public Health Service to reduce from thirty-seven to sixteen the number of people reporting to the surgeon general. Califano based his approach on the view that a department such as HEW "required a central mechanism through which all significant policy would flow."[12] He created an Executive Secretariat that would provide a way to coordinate and control this policy flow.

Califano attempted to deal with what he viewed as responsibilities that "provoked wide-ranging and intense controversy," noting that the department contained programs and policies that evoked strong and conflicting views. He commented that "[t]here was no way for an active Secretary to avoid controversy. Even when disagreements arose, however, it was important to try to keep the confidence of the array of competing, and often conflicting, interests that confronted HEW."[13] Disagreements with the White House (particularly involving the movement of the education programs out of the department) limited the anticipated impact of Califano's strategy.

Management efforts within the department thus reflected an approach that emphasized control, monitoring, consistency in operations and approaches, and clarity about lines of authority. From the 1960s on, most secretaries of the department searched for management systems that provided policy leadership and, as well, offered a way for them to oversee departmental administrative matters and programs. In a few cases, efforts at management reform have accentuated attempts to identify interdependencies and shared issues across program elements. Most efforts, however, emphasized modes of control of the separate elements within the department.

Despite these efforts at centralization, that strategy did not appear to be an effective way of dealing with external and internal realities surrounding the department.[14] These realities included the following elements.

Diversity and size of operating programs: The large number of programs contained within the HHS umbrella represents a diverse array of objectives, cultures, and approaches. Each of the components within the department has its own history, needs, and methods. Attempting to homogenize them within a centralized unit—even for planning purposes—dilutes their strengths and their unique values.

Vague, difficult goals: The department's programs embody goals that are often contradictory, vague, not unified, and difficult to measure. Efforts to find goals and objectives that link separate programs too often result in situations in which controversies embodied in the programs are ignored or posed in highly abstract forms.

Fragmented accountability structures: The accountability structures that frame the programs within the department mirror the fragmented nature of the American policy-making system. Units within the department are responsible to a number of separate budget, oversight, and authorizing congressional committees that represent different perspectives on programs. Some of these committees and subcommittees have established detailed expectations for the implementation of programs under their control. Departmental units are also subject to the expectations that are defined by the Executive Office of the President, particularly the Office of Management and Budget and the domestic policy staff, which often differ from congressional expectations.

Fragmented program authority: Some of the programs within the department have more in common with programs found in other departments or agencies than they do with other HHS programs. The congressional predilection to fragment program authority has created a crazy quilt array of program responsibilities across the federal government.

Different program responsibilities: HHS has responsibility for programs that contain a wide range of administrative and policy mechanisms. Some of the programs that are implemented by HHS actually require department staff to perform the work or deliver the services. Others involve providing funds (as block grants, as discretionary grants, or in other forms) to others, particularly states and communities, who deliver the services.

Controversial issues: Many of the policy issues that are contained within the HHS portfolio represent some of the most controversial domestic policy issues in the society. Issues such as government expenditures for abortion, welfare reform, and financing of health services evoke a variety of views and reflect different perspectives on politics and policies. Although the department may seek to take a clear position on such issues, the external forces often work in different directions. In addition, the department's role involving these issues may be as a funder of programs that are delivered by other levels of government, not as the actual deliverer itself.

Diverse constituencies: The diversity of programs within the department is paralleled by an even more diverse set of constituencies that follow the details of decisions involving their concerns. Constituency or interest groups focused on a specific set of programs often represent different approaches to those programs. The department attempts to deal with multiple perspectives on a program area. In such a situation, ambiguity rather than clarity often serves the department well.

Multiple policy perspectives: The controversies found within the society sometimes have been reflected within the department itself. In the past, individuals appointed to top political roles represented diverse policy and political agendas. It was not uncommon to have a secretary committed to one perspective on an issue and a deputy secretary or assistant secretary believing in a very different approach. When this occurred, it was difficult to reach agreement on policy directions, and loyalty to a single agenda defined by the secretary was difficult to achieve.

Conflicting policy approaches: At times the diverse program components within the department represent different approaches to the same policy problem. When there is disagreement on the most effective way to address policy issues, various program elements may be charged with quite different (indeed, sometimes conflicting) approaches. For example, health research agencies may develop effective treatment forms that are not reimbursed by the agencies charged with financing services. This evokes conflict among the units for the preeminent role on the issue.

Staff-line competition: The growth of an active and large Office of the Secretary staff, with its various components, led to competition between the program units and the Office of the Secretary for influence and the secretary's ear. Program units sometimes perceived the role of the Office of the Secretary to be one of second-guessing the decisions of the operating components and overturning their recommendations. As the Office of the Secretary grew larger in size, the various staff units had increased ability to monitor the program unit decisions more closely and to substitute their own technical judgment for that of the operating unit staff. This led to practices in which program units sought ways to avoid interacting with the staff components and, instead, learned how to minimize their impact on the program.

The roles that are currently found within the Office of the Secretary have remained fairly consistent over time. Staff offices in the Office of the Secretary include management, budget, planning and evaluation, legislation, public affairs, the general counsel's office, the office for civil rights, the inspector general, regional and intergovernmental offices. Although the names of the units have remained much the same over the years, the size of these units and the extent of their responsibilities have increased and then decreased over time.

Gaming filtering units: The creation of filtering units (that is, units that are established to filter information and package decision memos before they reach the secretary) did not guarantee that decisions would be more effective nor did they provide a way to represent varying perspectives within the department.[15] At times the program units found ways to bypass these efforts or bring such filtering units into the process very late in the game.

The HHS organization at the turn of the twenty-first century continues to have much in common with the HEW that Rufus Miles described, reflecting the social revolutions that continue to take place within the American society. The department continues to grapple with civil rights questions, dramatic changes in the health care delivery system, and the consumer rights revolution, but it also has to confront major shifts in the role of government, particularly the role of the federal government.

Although department secretaries face a formidable set of management issues, it is worth looking closely at one: how to define the role of the Office of the Secretary and its relationship to the operating components of the agency. The secretary is seen as the official "head" of the agency and thus held publicly accountable for the actions of the programs within it. Simultaneously, Congress and the public frequently focus on the individual operating components when specific action is demanded. The department is then expected to respond to two sets of expectations that call for inconsistent strategies: *centralization* in the Office of the Secretary and *decentralization* in its operating programs.

THE HHS PORTFOLIO CIRCA 2001: THE PIECES IN THE PORTFOLIO

As the previous section has indicated, few public agencies in the world are as complex as the U.S. Department of Health and Human Services. The management challenges that are posed by this public organization have worried administrators and policy makers since the department was officially created as the Department of Health, Education, and Welfare in April 1953, converting the Federal Security Agency (an agency that contained a range of programs) to a cabinet-level department.

Today the department's more than three hundred programs cover a vast array of activities in medical and social science research; food and drug safety; financial assistance and health care for low-income, elderly, and disabled Americans; child support enforcement; maternal and infant health; substance abuse treatment and prevention; and services for older Americans. The range of these programs means that the activities found within the department affect the health and welfare of nearly all individuals residing in the United States.

The $423 billion budget for fiscal year 2001 is implemented by 63,100 employees. HHS is the largest grant-making agency in the federal government, providing some 60,000 grants per year. It is also the nation's largest health insurer, handling more than 800 million claims per year.

The following descriptions give an indication of the responsibilities of each of the major program components within the department. From these descriptions it can be seen that each of the elements has unique attributes, in regard to both the kinds of services it supports and the goals of the effort. More detailed information about programs within the department can be found in the Annotated List of Abbreviations and Terms at the front of the book and in Appendix 4.

Public Health Service Operating Divisions

National Institutes of Health (NIH). — The world's premier medical research organization, the NIH supports some 35,000 research projects nationwide in such diseases as cancer, Alzheimer's, diabetes, arthritis, heart ailments, and AIDS. It includes eighteen separate health institutes, the National Center for Complementary and Alternative Medicine, and the National Library of Medicine. Established in 1887 as the Hygienic Laboratory, Staten Island, New York. Its headquarters are in Bethesda, Maryland.
Employees: 17,046.
FY '01 budget: $20.5 billion.

Food and Drug Administration (FDA). — The FDA ensures the safety of foods and cosmetics, and the safety and efficacy of pharmaceuticals, biological products, and medical devices—products that represent 25 cents out of every dollar in U.S. consumer spending. Established in 1906, its headquarters are in Rockville, Maryland.
Employees: 9,333.
FY '01 budget: $1.2 billion.

Centers for Disease Control and Prevention (CDC). — The CDC is the leading federal agency responsible for protecting the health of the American public through monitoring disease trends, investigating outbreaks of diseases, monitoring health and injury risks, fostering safe and healthful environments, and implementing illness and injury control and prevention interventions. The CDC was established in 1946 as the Communicable Disease Center. Its headquarters are in Atlanta, Georgia.
Employees: 7,511.
FY '01 budget: $4.1 billion.

Indian Health Service (IHS). — The IHS has 37 hospitals, 60 health centers, 3 school health centers, and 46 health stations. It also assists 34 urban Indian health centers. In addition, through transfers of IHS services, programs, and facilities, tribes administer an additional 13 hospitals, 160 health centers, 3 school health centers, 76 health stations, and 160 Alaska village clinics. Services are provided to nearly 1.5 million American Indians and Alaska Natives of 557 federally recognized tribes through a workforce of approximately 14,500 federal employees and additional tribal and urban Indian health employees. Annually there are about 69,000 hospital admissions and 7 million outpatient visits, 4 million community health representative client contacts, and 2.4 million dental services. The IHS was established in 1924 (mission transferred from the Interior Department in 1955). Its headquarters are in Rockville, Maryland.

Employees: 14,826.

FY '01 budget: $3.1 billion.

Health Resources and Services Administration (HRSA). — HRSA provides access to essential health services for people who are poor, who are uninsured, or who live in rural and urban neighborhoods where health care is scarce. HRSA-funded health centers provide comprehensive primary and preventive medical care to more than 9 million patients each year at more than 3,000 sites nationwide. Working in partnership with many state and community organizations, HRSA also supports programs that ensure healthy mothers and children, increase the number and diversity of health care professionals in underserved communities, and provide supportive services for people fighting HIV/AIDS through the Ryan White Care Act. HRSA was established in 1982, bringing together several already-existing programs. Its headquarters are in Rockville, Maryland.

Employees: 2,240.

FY '01 budget: $6.2 billion.

Substance Abuse and Mental Health Services Administration (SAMHSA). — SAMHSA works to improve the quality and availability of substance abuse prevention, addiction treatment, and mental health services. It provides funding to the states to support and maintain substance abuse and mental health services through federal block grants. Targeted Capacity Expansion grants provide mayors and other town and county officials with resources to address emerging drug abuse trends and mental health service needs and related public health problems, including HIV/AIDS, at the earliest possible stages. The agency funds hundreds of programs nationwide to increase the use of and improve prevention and treatment methods shown by research to be effective through "Knowledge Development and Application" grants. Established in 1992, its predecessor agency was the Alcohol, Drug Abuse and Mental Health Administration, established in 1974. SAMHSA's headquarters are in Rockville, Maryland.

Employees: 624.

FY '01 budget: $2.9 billion.

Agency for Healthcare Research and Quality (AHRQ). — The AHRQ is the leading agency charged with supporting research that is designed to improve the quality of health care, reduce its cost, improve patient safety, address medical errors, and broaden access to essential services. AHRQ sponsors and conducts research that provides evidence-based information on health care outcomes; quality; and cost, use, and access. The information helps health care decision makers, patients, clinicians, health system leaders, and policy makers make more informed decisions and improve the quality of health care services. Established in 1989, its headquarters are in Rockville, Maryland.

Employees: 294.

FY '01 budget: $270 million.

Human Services Operating Divisions

Center for Medicare and Medicaid Services (CMS). — Formerly the Health Care Financing Administration (HCFA), CMS administers the Medicare and Medicaid programs, which provide health care to about one in every four Americans. Medicare provides health insurance for more than 39 million elderly and disabled Americans. Medicaid, a joint federal-state program, provides health coverage for more than 34 million low-income persons, including nearly 18 million children, and nursing home coverage for low-income elderly. CMS also administers the new Children's Health Insurance Program through approved state plans that cover more than 2.2 million children. CMS was established in 1977 as HCFA. It has its headquarters in Baltimore, Maryland.

Employees: 4,435.

FY '01 budget: $339.4 billion.

Administration for Children and Families (ACF). — ACF is responsible for some sixty programs that promote the economic and social well-being of families, children, individuals, and communities. It administers the state-federal welfare program, Temporary Assistance to Needy Families, begun in September 1998, that provides assistance to an estimated 7.3 million persons, including 6.3 million children. It also administers the national child support enforcement system, collecting some $15.5 billion in fiscal year 1999 in payments from noncustodial parents. The Head Start program, too, serving more than 877,000 preschool children, is under its aegis. In addition it provides funds to assist low-income families in paying for child care, supports state programs to provide for foster care and adoption assistance, and funds programs to prevent child abuse and domestic violence. Established in 1991, it brought together several already-existing programs. Its headquarters are in Washington, D.C.

Employees: 1,532.

FY '01 budget: $43.4 billion.

Administration on Aging (AoA). — The Administration on Aging is the federal focal point and advocate agency for older persons and their concerns. AoA administers key federal programs mandated under various titles of the Older Americans Act. These programs help vulnerable older persons remain in their own homes by providing supportive services, including nutrition programs like home-delivered meals (Meals on Wheels). Other programs offer older Americans opportunities to enhance their health and to be active contributors to their families, communities, and the nation. AoA works closely with its nationwide network of regional offices and state and area agencies on aging to plan, coordinate, and develop community-level systems of services that meet the unique needs of individual older persons and their caregivers. AoA collaborates with federal agencies, national organizations, and representatives of business to ensure that, whenever possible, their programs and resources are targeted to older persons and coordinated with those of the network on aging.

Employees: 121.

FY '01 budget: $1.1 billion.

In addition, the Program Support Center, a service-for-fee organization, uses a pioneering business enterprise approach to provide government support services throughout HHS as well as other departments and federal agencies. Administrative operations, financial management, and human resources are oriented toward problem solving and are highly responsive to customer needs.

CONCLUSION

As a result of preparing for the position of HHS secretary, Raymond Wilson recognizes that he will never be able to keep all the details of the various programs at his fingertips. The materials that he has developed will largely serve as reference sources that he can call on in the future. He knows he will have to live with two conflicting perspectives: he is required to view the department as a unified entity yet treat it as an array of very diffuse programs. The challenge for him is to adopt a strategy that reconciles two conflicting imperatives. The juggling metaphor seems apt. He wants to be seen as a capable manager, but he also wants both the HHS staff and the multiple publics and groups that are a part of the department's world to perceive him as a leader and an individual with political clout.

Notes

1. Rufus E. Miles Jr., *The Department of H.E.W.* (New York: Praeger, 1974), v. This book was one of a series of volumes on federal departments.

2. Ibid., 1–2, 64.

3. Ibid., 3–4.

4. Ibid., 299.

5. Ibid., 300.

6. See discussion of reorganization efforts in Beryl A. Radin and Willis D. Hawley, *The Politics of Federal Reorganization: Creating the U.S. Department of Education* (New York: Pergamon Press, 1988), 22.

7. Ibid., 24.

8. This is drawn from Beryl A. Radin, "Managing Decentralized Departments: The Case of the U.S. Department of Health and Human Services," Grant Report, PricewaterhouseCoopers Endowment for the Business of Government, October 1999.

9. U.S. General Accounting Office, Report to the Congress, *Management of HHS: Using the Office of the Secretary to Enhance Departmental Effectiveness,* GAO HRD 90-15, February 1990, 3.

10. Quoted in ibid., 20.

11. Ibid., 1.

12. Joseph A. Califano Jr., *Governing America: An Insider's Report from the White House and the Cabinet* (New York: Simon and Schuster, 1981), 43, 44.

13. Califano, *Governing America,* 22–23.

14. HHS is not the only cabinet agency that contains diverse elements. However, the size and scope of the programs within HHS make the job of the secretary incredibly demanding.

15. Executive Secretariats have been created in a number of cabinet departments as a way to deal with this process. These offices vary in terms of their influence on the decision-making process, depending on the style of the secretary and the personal relationship between the person heading that office and the secretary.

Accountability and the
Policy Lens

AS HE GOES through the process of sorting out the HHS programs, Raymond Wilson finds that he is creating categories of programs that reflect patterns and similarities across the department's portfolio. He is struck by the incredible variegation in the federal role within the department. Some of the programs were delivered directly by federal officials, who had very different perspectives and backgrounds. The department's personnel roster included physicians, social workers, and specialists from a variety of professions who actually provided direct services to citizens. Other programs were staffed by federal officials who focused on the transfer of money and other resources to state and local governments, nonprofit groups, and even to the private sector.

The individuals within the department were responsible for many different functions, ranging from providing technical assistance to creating data systems, supporting training efforts, and improving management capacities. Some of the program staff were responsible for regulating the actions of others, operating in a somewhat adversarial relationship with those groups and individuals. Still others worked closely as partners with nonprofit organizations or state or local groups to accomplish federal goals. The department contained programs in which the federal role was disbursing block grants, largely to states, where the federal role was very limited. In other programs the federal role was quite directive and explicitly called on those who received funds to carry out specific functions in specific ways. Some of the HHS programs reflected a commitment by the federal government to pay for or actually deliver services; others, by contrast, were largely funded by others.

Although some of the differences that Wilson identifies resulted from the form that a program took, other differences reflected strong and distinct cultures of units within the department. Even in the health programs—the programs that Wilson knows best—he recognizes that he cannot assume that the Medicare and Medicaid programs (programs that require expertise in health financing) have much in common with the health research efforts found in the NIH or the CDC. The culture of science and the high professional status of health researchers enabled the NIH and the CDC to operate independently.

He had thought that the accountability literature might help him think about these issues, but this turned out not to be the case. Another review of the materials prepared by his staff indicates that the literature ignores what he is learning. Rather than differentiating between the accountability expectations tied to different program forms, the literature tended to the one-size-fits-all approach—ignoring variation in accountability expectations depending on the policy form involved.

As Wilson continues his preparation for the confirmation hearings, he asks himself several questions:

• Are there more effective ways to sort out the many programs within the department's portfolio?
• Should the secretary emphasize the program design, its policy area, or its possible level of controversy?
• How can the secretary respect the individual cultures, the professional expertise found within the different programs, and the autonomy of the program units and, at the same time, find a way to deal with the programmatic overlaps among these units?

THIS CHAPTER focuses on the relationship between policy design and form and the accountability relationships that flow from it. It includes a discussion of types of federal aid, different strategies employed, various forms of policy design and policy goals, the extent of the federal role, and different cultures that make up HHS. The variety of program forms within the department's portfolio resembles the range of items that the Flying Karamazov Brothers juggled; it concocts an image similar to the variety of items represented by a cat, Jell-O, and a car part.

The three hundred programs included in the HHS portfolio create a formidable obstacle to anyone attempting to manage the department. The complexity of managing HHS is not only related to the number of programs on the secretary's plate but also to the diversity of the substantive focus of these programs.

The programs also vary tremendously in their design, their relationship to those who are funded by them, and in the policy cultures that are attached to them. Any attempt to develop a single approach to these programs confronts very different realities. Some of the past HHS secretaries have emphasized commonalities rather than differences among the program units and, as a result, find themselves dealing with change in abstract and general terms. In order to deal with all the programs at once, the secretary's decisions must be general enough to apply to the wide-ranging array of programs. The one-size-fits-all approach rarely focuses on substantive policy or the programmatic results of action.

The programs within the HHS portfolio date back to efforts enacted during the twentieth century. Prior to that period, the national bureaucracy was small, with minimal national-state overlap.[1] Deil Wright argues that the period 1914 to 1921 was a landmark era when about a dozen grants-in-aid were enacted to support, among other areas, maternal and child health. The programs that were enacted during this period often included apportionment formulas for fund distribution among the states, requirements that states match the federal contribution, advance approval by the federal government of state plans, and requirements for planning, administrative practices, and reporting. Although there were legal challenges to what was viewed as an expansion of the powers of the national government involving maternal and child health programs, the Supreme Court ruled in several cases that the national government has the power to spend funds for specific programs.

Since that period, federal aid has expanded greatly in several ways: in the number and size of programs as well as in the variety of forms that the aid takes. This expansion has been daunting. Despite the rhetoric calling for cutbacks in federal programs that began during the Nixon administration, much of the growth has actually occurred since that time.

TYPES OF FEDERAL AID

There are many ways of classifying federal aid programs. One useful typology looks at the type of financial authorization attached to the program—whether that authorization is for loans or grants. *Loans* provide funds to individuals and groups with the expectation that they will be paid back in the future; they are usually attached to specific and defined purposes or projects. *Grants* take different forms but also provide money to individuals or groups with limits or restrictions attached to them. Grants are often divided into two types—categorical grants and block grants. Categorical grants are designed for specific purposes and often require the recipient to spend the funds in specific ways. Block grants are also created to meet specific needs but provide discretion to the recipient in the way that the funds are spent.

Historically, grants—usually called grants-in-aid—have been the dominant form of federal aid. According to Deil Wright, federal grants have several distinguishing features.

- Congressional authorizing legislation establishes a grant program for a specified number of years or on a continuing basis.
- Annual appropriations, which may be less than authorized amounts, provide funds for distribution among states or their subdivisions, (a) usually in accordance with a legislatively prescribed formula, (b) generally contingent on state or local matching funds, and (c) based on conditions that Congress, the president, or executive agencies specify and that are agreed to by the recipient.
- Allocation, supervision, review, approval, and audit responsibilities over the receiving units are performed by a federal administrative agency.
- Funds are allocated in the first instance to units of government rather than to individuals, nonprofit and semipublic groups, or private firms. But the nongovernmental entities (or third parties) may . . . be significant actors and recipients in the implementation process.[2]

Although historically the grants that exhibit these features have taken the form of categorical grants focused on specific goals as well as the means to accomplish them (that is, specific limits or restrictions on how the grant funds may be used), block grants have become increasingly present since the first formal block grant was funded in 1966 (the Partnership for Health Act).[3] Wright distinguishes a block grant from a categorical grant in five ways:

1. Recipients of block grant monies have more discretion in deciding what specific project or purposes will be funded within a broad program or functional area.
2. The planning, reporting, auditing, and other "red-tape" aspects are considerably reduced for block grants, with the intent of reducing grantor supervision and control.
3. Block grant funds are dispensed on the basis of a formula, so that the intended recipient units will be more knowledgeable and certain of the aid amounts, and the national administrative agency will not have discretion to decide the amount of funds allocated to a state or local units.
4. Eligibility provisions are fairly precise for block grants. They tend to favor units of general government as opposed to special-district governments, and favor state and local generalists over program specialists.
5. Financing provisions in block grants usually specify very low state and local matching funds, or none.[4]

For example, the Preventive Health and Health Services Block Grant, administered by the Centers for Disease Control (CDC), provides all states that wish to participate with funds for preventive health services not covered by other grants to reduce preventable morbidity and mortality and improve quality of life. States are given significant flexibility in deciding how funding can be used to meet state preventive health priorities. The block grant allows states to pay for specific programs (such as programs for community and school-based fluoridation programs and rodent control) as well as the development of new health data systems. Although the block grant does give states significant discretion, it requires that states create an advisory committee that is responsible for holding public hearings and making recommendations regarding the state plan.

Another CDC program provides funds to all states for Breast and Cervical Cancer Mortality Prevention Activities. Unlike a block grant, however, this categorical grant program specifies that states use the funds for the development of comprehensive programs that are defined by the CDC. Thus the CDC supports activities at the state and national level in the areas of screening, referral, and follow-up services; quality assurance; public and provider education, surveillance, and collaboration; and partnership development.

The CDC's Prevention Centers program is an example of a competitive grant program. The CDC provides grants to academic institutions (schools of medicine, public health, or osteopathy) to fund applied research designed to develop new and innovative strategies in health promotion and disease prevention. Each grantee is expected to work with state and local health departments and other agencies to conduct research on a particular theme.

Each of these three programs has a different set of expectations in regard to the HHS role. These differences tend to be defined from the perspective of the federal agency. Still another way of conceptualizing the variety of programs flows from the recipient's perspective. Recipients of federal aid usually strive to ensure that they have significant discretion in the use of the funds. Thus, formula-based grants provide more discretion for the recipient than do project grants.

ISSUES OF POLICY DESIGN

The determination of the form of federal assistance usually occurs during the stage in which policy specifics are formulated and debated. Several predictable questions are asked during this stage—the policy design stage—that affect the relationship between the national government and the recipients of the federal monies:[5]

1. Should the government be involved at all in this issue?
2. If so, at what level of government?
3. For what aspect of the issue should that level (or levels) be responsible?
4. What mechanisms should be used to carry out that responsibility (for example, financial grants, technical assistance, implementation requirements, evaluation requirements)?

5. What patterns and rules should be used to allocate those resources?
6. How will information resources be transacted across units to achieve desired outcomes?

There are many ways of categorizing the variations in government financing, implementation, and effect across different functional or policy areas. Theodore Lowi's typology, used in several analyses within the United States, differentiates between (1) redistributive, (2) regulatory, and (3) distributive or developmental policies.[6]

Redistributive policies have been defined in several ways. In one definition, such policies are simply those that derive from zero-sum politics: some groups win and some lose in the pushing and pulling of the political system. In the intergovernmental area, however, redistribution often refers to the national government's responsibility for policy areas that were previously under state or local control or were not matters for public action. Policies in this area might take the form of targeting specific population groups that are viewed as particularly needy or establishment of rights for groups that require protection. For example, at various times the United States has adopted policies that provide income and service support for citizens in poverty or provide special education funds for Native Americans or children who have a limited knowledge of English. Methods of redistribution may focus on individuals (for example, income transfer programs or vouchers) or on groups. Within this latter category, programs may emphasize the territorial discrepancies within the country (for example, disparities between regions) or particular groups within a geographic area. In these instances, redistribution occurs between levels of government rather than between government and an individual.

One such program is the Health Careers Opportunity Program, administered by the Health Resources and Services Administration (HRSA). This program is designed to increase the number of individuals in the health professions from disadvantaged backgrounds. The program seeks to build diversity by allowing students to enhance their academic skills to successfully compete, enter, and graduate from health professions programs. The program focuses on the disparities between the percentage of African Americans, Hispanics, and Native Americans in the U.S. population and their representation in health professions schools. This is a competitive grant program that supports projects around the country.

Another example of a redistributive policy is found in the Health Centers program also administered by HRSA. This effort is designed to serve the millions of people in the United States who lack access to primary care provided in geographically underserved areas. Working in tandem with the National Health Service Corps, these efforts focus on pregnant women and infants, the homeless, substance abusers, migrant farm workers, the elderly, and others who lack health care. Grants are made to specific centers to provide these services.

The Low Income Heating and Energy Assistance Program (LIHEAP), administered by the Administration for Children and Families, assists eligible low-income households in meeting the heating or cooling portion of their residential energy needs. The law defines low-income households as those with incomes that do not exceed the greater of 150 percent of the poverty level or 60 percent of state median income. LIHEAP grantees have the flexibility of setting their income eligibility at or below this maximum standard, as long as they do not set income eligibility below 110 percent of the poverty level.

LIHEAP agencies must conduct outreach activities that ensure that eligible households, especially households with members who are elderly, disabled, or with a young child and those with high home energy costs in relation to income, are aware that LIHEAP assistance is available. The availability of LIHEAP assistance is dependent in large part upon the amount of federal funds that LIHEAP grantees receive each year.

LIHEAP agencies may also require that low-income households meet additional criteria to be eligible to receive assistance. Depending on the LIHEAP grantee, LIHEAP funds can be used for heating or cooling assistance, energy crisis intervention, or low-cost weatherization and other energy-related home repair.

Regulatory policies impose limitations or control the behavior of certain individuals or groups for society's benefit. These limitations can be imposed on individuals, private groups, or other governments. These limitations are often referred to as *mandates*, whereby grantees are provided funds conditioned by their agreement to accept certain requirements or standards. In the intergovernmental area national standards can be imposed on other levels of government through direct orders; crosscutting requirements (such as nondiscrimination, environmental protection); crossover sanctions (linking the requirements in one to the benefits in another); and partial preemption (when national standards are created but administration is delegated to states with equivalent policies).[7]

The Food and Drug Administration plays a regulatory role in many areas, including food, drugs for human use, and medical devices. The FDA has adopted a food safety program developed nearly thirty years ago for astronauts and is applying it to seafood. The agency intends to eventually use it for much of the U.S. food supply. Traditionally, industry and regulators have depended on spot-checks of manufacturing conditions and random sampling of final products to ensure safe food. This approach, however, tends to be reactive, rather than preventive, and can be less efficient than the new system.

The new system is known as Hazard Analysis and Critical Control Point, or HACCP (pronounced hassip). Many of its principles already are in place in the FDA-regulated low-acid canned food industry. And, in a 1995 final rule that took effect in December 1997, the FDA established HACCP for the seafood industry. Also, the FDA has incorporated HACCP into its Food Code, a document that gives guidance to and serves as model legislation for state and territorial agencies that license and inspect food service establishments, retail food stores, and food-vending operations in the United States.

To help determine the degree to which such regulations would be feasible, the agency has conducted pilot HACCP programs with volunteer food companies. The programs have involved cheese, frozen dough, breakfast cereals, salad dressing, fresh and pasteurized juices, bread, flour, and other products.

Another regulatory policy that is administered within the HHS involves nursing homes. The Centers for Medicare and Medicaid Services (CMS) is charged with the oversight of the health and safety of about 1.6 million older Americans and people with disabilities who receive care in approximately 16,700 nursing homes that are funded through the Medicare or Medicaid programs. Since new regulations were put in place in 1995, the health and safety of nursing homes have improved. For example, the inappropriate use of physical restraints has been cut by more than half, and the number of nursing home residents receiving hearing aids is up 30 percent. Over the past years, efforts have been put into place to crack down on poor-quality nursing homes and ensure high-quality care. When the agency finds violations in nursing homes, it can work with the Justice Department to level fines against these institutions.[8]

Distributive or developmental policies have concentrated on clearly focused benefits or results. They have been defined as having the following characteristics:

- Provide subsidies to encourage private activities
- Convey tangible government benefits to individuals, groups, or firms
- Appear to produce only winners, not losers
- Are typically based on decisions guided by short-run consequences
- Involve a high degree of cooperation and mutually rewarding logrolling
- Are marked by low visibility
- Are fairly stable over time[9]

The Organ Transplantation Program, administered by HRSA, is an example of a developmental policy. It is a program that is charged with coordinating organ donation efforts nationally, promoting organ and tissue donation, and supporting efforts directed at an improved understanding of the consent and referral processes that take place between hospital and referral personnel and families.

The Adoption Opportunities program, administered by the Administration for Children and Families, is also a policy that has a developmental agenda. This program eliminates barriers to adoption and helps to find permanent families for children who would benefit by adoption, particularly children with special needs. The program promotes the development and implementation of a national adoption and foster care data-gathering and analysis system; a national adoption information exchange system; an adoption training and technical assistance program; and an increase in the placements in adoptive families of minority children who are in foster care. It also seeks to increase post-legal adoption services for families who have adopted children with special needs.

In many cases, policies emerge from the political process containing a combination of these policy types. Thus the goals of the programs contain mixed strategies, making accountability expectations more complex. Coalitions are devised to maximize political support, not to enhance policy design coherence. To achieve these coalitions, parts of policy proposals may be cobbled together. Thus the policy has elements of both redistributive and distributive goals. Some argue that this system is not workable and, instead, call for the clear delineation of type of program by level of government.[10]

Lowi is not alone in attempting to explain variations in policy making. David Price focused on the legislative policy-making area and argued that Congress is likely to intervene when public knowledge and interest in an issue is high and conflict (that is, disagreements between groups) is low.[11] William Gormley and Cristina Boccuti used the Price typology to explain the highly diverse issue portfolio within HHS, particularly within the Centers for Medicare and Medicaid Services.[12] They note that some issues have strong public support, whereas others are highly conflictive. They also note that issues change over time.

MULTIPLE STRATEGIES

Not only are the goals and objectives of programs mixed, but many of the HHS programs contain a combination of strategies and approaches to designing the federal role. These include the following.

- *Provision of resources for treatment or services.* They may be targeted at specific client groups, such as the elderly or children.
- *Support of research.* Research efforts may include either basic or applied programs. In addition, programs may be designed to support dissemination of findings.
- *Development of demonstration efforts.* In an area where effective methods of intervention are not known, the federal role may be to support various approaches to deal with the particular issue.
- *Requirements for or support of evaluations.* The federal government may undertake an evaluation program itself or require grantees to develop their own evaluation efforts.
- *Data collection, development of data systems, and information provision.* Although the federal government may not be involved in supporting specific programs, it may provide assistance to others through the development of data systems. In other cases, the federal role may require data collection.

- *Prevention programs.* These are particularly present in public health programs where the federal role is to devise methods and strategies to prevent problems from occurring.
- *Public education.* These efforts may be devised for the general population or targeted to a specific group of beneficiaries.
- *Regulation.* In these programs, the federal role is to ensure enforcement of specific standards and requirements.
- *Development of standards.* In these programs, the federal government may work with others to create a set of standards for a specific program area.
- *Devising of partnerships.* The federal role may be as a facilitator or broker to ensure that various groups within the society are involved in an effort.
- *Support of or requirement for training.* This is most common in a new policy area or where various groups within the society have not been represented in an effort.
- *Provision or support of technical assistance.* The federal role may be to provide technical assistance to grantees to assist them in carrying out a program. This may be done directly (for example, support of technical specialists) or by facilitating peer-to-peer technical assistance.
- *Support of outreach efforts to improve access to services.* This may occur when a new program is undertaken and grantees do not know how to facilitate use of that program.
- *Improvement in state or local infrastructure.* This strategy is often called capacity development and provides funds for state or local grantees to upgrade their ability to deliver a program.
- *Improvement in the management of programs.* Funds may be made available to grantees (both state and local agencies and nonprofit groups) who have not been able to effectively manage a program.

THE EXTENT OF THE FEDERAL ROLE

It is not surprising, given the political, economic, and social culture of the United States, that most of the major domestic programs and policies provide an important implementation role for states, localities, or even nongovernmental sectors. It is these actors, not federal agencies or staff, who actually deliver the services to eligible individuals. As one former HHS secretary commented, "I am not responsible for delivering services to people; I deliver dollars and regulations to others who deliver those services." This reality has its roots in the nation's skepticism about government action, its commitment to pluralism, and the diversity of settings within the United States. The tradition of American pragmatism has pushed for a constant redefinition of what is appropriate for the national government to do— but it has frequently expanded the national role by providing new implementation responsibilities for the delivery of services to other levels of government.

At least three elements involving implementation are worthy of emphasis: (1) the diversity of predictable state responses to an initiative; (2) expectations about national commitment to some kind of action; and (3) the role to be played by the national bureaucracy responsible for implementing the program. When others—particularly state agencies—are involved in the crafting of a policy or program, they become a part of the accountability system surrounding that effort.

If variability can be anticipated across the United States in the implementation process, it is difficult to determine the appropriate expectations for a national program or policy. There are several approaches to this dilemma. Some students of the implementation process suggest that national policy should be viewed as a set of general principles or values that guide those who carry out the program. Others, by contrast, believe that the principles of accountability in a government system demand that the national government find ways to hold others accountable for implementation of programs or policies.

When viewed from the perspective of the federal government, the significance of a program may be measured in terms of the federal dollars appropriated for that effort. But when viewed from the perspective of the grantee, the federal funds may not reach the same level of significance. Perhaps the most dramatic example of this problem is found in the Mental Health Performance Partnership Block Grant, administered by the Substance Abuse and Mental Health Services Administration. Although this block grant has grown to more than $400 million, the impact of the funds is relatively small from the perspective of the states. In no state do the services supported by federal dollars rise to more than 11 percent. In this instance, the federal role is viewed in developmental terms, supporting some services but—more important—leveraging changes to support a comprehensive community mental health services planning system in all states. Although SAMHSA may have a set of goals for its funds, it has limited ability to create this change. In this case, the discretion and flexibility that follow any block grant program are intensified because the federal dollars are only a small percentage of the funds that support the programs. Similarly, the federal funds that are provided for case management services for the elderly, administered by the Administration on Aging, provide less than 20 percent of the funds that are expended for the service. In both of these cases, the real implementation decisions are made by the state agencies with both fiscal and programmatic responsibility for the majority of the program.

In another program area, the federal role is also constrained because of requirements for states to match federal dollars. Medicaid, administered by the CMS, is financed by approximately 43 percent of its money from the states and 57 percent from the federal government. But for many states, the Medicaid budget is one of the largest elements in the state budget and thus it receives concentrated attention within the state decision-making process. State Medicaid agencies also have significant discretion in establishing eligibility under the program but continue to be directly involved with the CMS in carrying out the goals for those who may be eligible for several programs, uninsured children, reduction in the use of physical restraints in long-term care facilities, development of linked Medicare and Medicaid data, and increasing immunization rates in Medicaid. Although it plays a role in the process, the federal agency is limited both programmatically and politically in its ability to devise what is thought to be a federal program.

By contrast, many HHS programs do support or provide most of the services to the target population and thus have more control over the implementation process. The Emergency Medical Services Program for Children, administered by HRSA, created a demonstration program that acknowledged that children's emergency care needs were not receiving adequate attention. The program was able to specify essential functions in this area, including training, communications, transportation, critical care facilities, and standard record keeping. The effort developed models for collaboration between a range of agencies and institutions.

Similarly, the Ryan White Program within HRSA began in 1990, providing funding to states and other public or private nonprofit entities to develop, organize, coordinate, and operate more effective and cost-efficient systems for the delivery of essential health care and support services to medically underserved individuals and families affected by the HIV disease. Grants were made for care and treatment services that contributed in large part to dramatic decreases in AIDS-related mortality in the United States by the end of the century.

In a few cases, the agency within HHS delivers the service itself and thus is not required to negotiate with or persuade others to carry out the federal goals. Many of the programs of the Indian Health Service are provided by health professionals directly employed by the federal government. In fact, until the passage of the Indian Self-Determination and Education Assistance Act in1975 and subsequent executive orders, all the services were provided by federal staff. As a result, IHS not only had responsibility for personnel matters dealing with staff but also with the details of maintaining facilities and providing clinical support for the delivery of both treatment and prevention services. Many of the people served by the IHS live in some of the most remote and poverty-stricken areas of the country, and these health services represent their only source of health care. Health services are provided to 1.43 million American Indian and Alaska Natives through 151 service units composed of 543 direct health care delivery facilities, including 49 hospitals; 209 health centers; 6 school health centers; and 279 health stations, satellite clinics, and Alaska village clinics. In addition, Indian tribes deliver IHS-funded services to their own communities, with more than 40 percent of IHS direct services budgets going to 12 hospitals, 149 health centers, 3 school health centers, and 233 health stations.

These examples illustrate the range of functions and tasks included within the HHS portfolio. Some programs require an arm's-length relationship between the federal program and the recipient of its funds because groups and individuals other than federal officials implement the program. Other programs, however, call for federal officials to focus on the details of implementation, since they are responsible for delivering the services.

It might be useful to think of these differences in terms of bureaucratic spheres—what Mark Yessian describes as general administration, program administration, and service delivery. Characteristics of general administration include broad management, planning, and policy-making orientations, all of which are highly influenced by elected or politically appointed officials, and emphasize functions performed by staff. Program administration, by contrast, focuses on a functional or programmatic perspective. The orientation is careerist and there is a heavy reliance upon a hierarchical, centralized mode of operation and a strong affiliation with interest groups. Service delivery calls for regular face-to-face contact with clients, a tension between bureaucratic and professional service roles, a high level of autonomy in service delivery roles, and strong affiliation with professional associations and unions.[13]

As this discussion has indicated, the form of a program and its assumptions about implementation roles create both opportunities and constraints for a federal policy official. Just because a program is found on the federal program roster, does not mean that federal staff have the ability to dictate how that effort will be implemented.

A COLLECTION OF SEPARATE CULTURES

James Q. Wilson noted that "many government agencies have multiple, competing cultures. Some manage the competition well, some do not." He also wrote that "[e]very organization has a culture, that is, a persistent, patterned way of thinking about the central tasks of and human relationships within an organization. Culture is to an organization what personality is to an individual. Like human culture generally, it is passed on from one generation to the next. It changes slowly, if at all."[14]

In a similar vein, Martin A. Levin and Mary Bryna Sanger commented that "[a]n organization's culture provides consistency and predictability for its members. It manifests what is important, valued, and accepted. It derives from a shared set of values and assumptions about a wide range of solutions to broad human issues. As such, cultures are infinitely variable from setting to setting."[15]

Given the diversity of programs and policies contained within HHS it is not surprising that this department contains a dramatically diverse collection of organizational cultures. For some, both inside and outside the department, this diversity is overwhelming; it is difficult to find a way to describe the nature of HHS as a whole because it contains such disparate elements. Yet others have found ways to build on the diverse cultures and use them effectively. For example, former

HHS secretary Donna Shalala has noted that there are times when it is very help-ful for the department to have more than one identity and that unique cultures can also increase credibility.[16]

Perhaps the best-defined culture within the department centers on the cluster of science agencies. Not only are these agencies staffed by highly trained and high-status professionals but they deal with issues that the public understands to be life and death questions. As Donna Shalala wrote,

> At HHS, I like to let the experts—especially physicians and scientists—speak directly to the public, because the great scientific agencies—CDC, the FDA, NIH, the National Cancer Institute (NCI), and the Public Health Service—are institutions trusted by the American people. The physician-scientists who head them, while appointed by the president, have enormous credibility . . . . When they appear before the public in white lab coats, the scientists in HHS present a very convincing argument.[17]

But it is not only the status of the scientific agencies that define their unique cultures. These agencies include staff who are bench scientists, focusing on their own research that is as rigorous and relevant as the external work that is sup-ported by federal dollars. The science agencies also are engaged in very different sorts of work. Commitment to the scientific method means that research that does not produce the expected results may, in the long run, turn out to be as im-portant (or, indeed, even more important) than the anticipated results. Scientific research does not move in a straight line; it meanders in many directions, and its results cannot be expected to follow the timeline defined by the institutions of governance. The accountability expectations that define these staff members are largely provided by their peers; the traditional legal and hierarchical forms dis-cussed earlier in the book play a much less important role in the way these scien-tists perceive their roles and organize their work.

There are other types of organizational cultures found within HHS. The Ma-ternal and Child Health (MCH) Services Block Grant, administered by HRSA, illustrates an organizational culture that transcends the boundaries of the federal agency. Although the MCH program is one of the oldest programs within the federal portfolio, operating for sixty years, its funding was converted to a block grant in 1981. At the same time such funding gave flexibility and discretion to the states, it also provided a way for the federal agency to account for the use of funds. Although other HHS programs have sought to balance these two compet-ing approaches, the culture of MCH allowed the development of a process that included both the state perspective and the federal perspective. Over the years, MCH federal staff had close relationships with MCH state and local staff. This set of relationships illustrates what is often called picket-fence federalism, where functional relationships have created "an alliance among like-minded program specialists or professionals, regardless of the level of government in which they serve."[18] Shared professional norms and, often, common training experiences have made it easier for the federal agency to develop a planning document in which states present their plans along a shared format.

One of the most common complaints by state and local governments is that the federal government attaches requirements to its funds that do not meet the needs of the nonfederal jurisdiction.[19] Indeed, this is one of the main arguments that has been used to justify the transformation of categorical program grants into block grant efforts. Although states and localities want to receive funds from the federal government, they frequently complain about the "strings" that are attached to those dollars.

In 1996 the MCH Bureau in the Health Resources and Services Administration of HHS began a process with states that would establish a set of mutually agreed-upon measures with data sources that would be used in the program. In the development phase of this process, the MCH Bureau created an external committee of thirty experts representing various interests in the maternal and child health field that would help set the overall direction for the process, provide technical expertise, and endorse the final results. Participants from associations and advocacy groups were expected to engage their own constituencies to ensure accurate representation. Review and comment from the state agency officials were solicited at various points during the process.

In March 1997 draft performance measures and guidance revision principles were presented at the annual meeting of the Association of Maternal and Child Health Programs; this meeting was attended by virtually all the relevant directors in the country. Eight representative states, chosen from seventeen volunteers, were selected to pilot test the measures for practicality and data collection issues. The consultation process that was used was approximately two years in duration; one year was spent on the development of the measures and one for running the pilot tests.

By the end of 1997, the MCH Bureau established eighteen national performance measures that were incorporated into the application and reporting guidance for the Title V block grant funds. The measures were categorized as capacity measures (ability to affect the delivery of services), process measures (related to service delivery), and risk factors (involving health problems). Each individual state also was required to establish and report on between seven and ten of its own supplemental performance measures to provide a more complete picture of the program within that state. In addition, the MCH Bureau set six national outcome measures—ultimate goals toward which the performance measures were directed and for which ultimate achievement depended on external factors beyond the control of the state grantee.

As a result of this process, states' MCH block grant applications and annual reports contain a wealth of information concerning state initiatives, state-supported programs, and other state-based responses designed to address their MCH needs. The electronic information system that has been developed in this program, based on the applications and reports, collects both qualitative and quantitative data that are useful to many audiences. Because of shared professional values across the intergovernmental system, the MCH program was able to devise a policy strategy that created a federal role even in a policy with high levels of discretion for states. This is an example of a program that was able to transcend the structure of the policy and develop an important role for federal officials.

Two programs administered by the Administration for Children and Families (ACF) also have developed strong and quite independent organizational cultures, sustained by their relationship to the groups they support. Both of these programs had their origins in the Office of Economic Opportunity (OEO), the agency that implemented the War on Poverty in the 1960s. The Office of Community Services is a direct descendent of the Community Action program, the effort that funded approximately three thousand neighborhood-based agencies and community development corporations across the country. These groups support various efforts that address the economic and social needs of the urban and rural poor at the local level.

The other program is Head Start—a child development program that has served low-income children and their families since 1965. It is administered by the Head Start Bureau in ACF. Grants are awarded by the ACF regional offices and the Head Start Bureau's American Indian and Migrant Program branches directly to local public agencies, private organizations, Indian tribes and school systems for the purpose of operating Head Start programs at the community level.

The Head Start program has a long tradition of delivering comprehensive and high-quality services designed to foster healthy development in low-income children. Head Start grantee and delegate agencies provide a range of individualized services in the areas of education and early childhood development; medical, dental, and mental health; nutrition; and parent involvement. In addition, the entire range of Head Start services is responsive and appropriate to each child's and family's developmental, ethnic, cultural, and linguistic heritage and experience.

Both the community action programs and Head Start have staff who have been committed to the mission of their respective agencies over the years, despite the structural shift from OEO to HHS. The sense of mission found in these organizations is supported by strong relationships with advocates of their approach throughout the country, often those who focus on problems of low-income families.

A sense of an autonomous organizational culture, thus, can be supported in several ways: by the social status of the staff and its work (as in the case of the science agencies), by the relationships that have been developed with those outside of the federal organization (as in MCH), and by an attempt to protect one's identity and mission in the face of policy and political turbulence (as in the case of the community action programs).

CONCLUSION

As these examples indicate, the programs within HHS vary tremendously in their design, in their relationship to those who are funded under them, and in the policy cultures that are attached to them. This variation creates a highly variegated set of expectations about accountability and makes it extremely difficult for a secretary of HHS to devise a single strategy to respond to these expectations. In this sense, the job of the secretary is best described as a juggling task.

Raymond Wilson's attempt to identify categories does help him understand the many variations and approaches within the department's portfolio. He realizes that differences in program design, the form and extent of the federal role, the policy area, and the level of controversy surrounding a program affect the accountability expectations attached to a specific program. Some programs give the secretary discretion and room to maneuver. Others lock him in, and he has to defer to the grantees. Even when it appears that the department has legal authority, in reality the political and professional power of the grantee limits that authority.

He also learns that he has to respect the individual cultures, professional expertise, and autonomy of the program units, even when he does not always agree with their approach. At the same time, he is aware that some units have overlapping programs. He realizes that as secretary he will have to be judicious in his choice of policies and areas that require his intervention.

Notes

1. Deil S. Wright, *Understanding Intergovernmental Relations,* 3d ed. (Pacific Grove, Calif.: Brooks/Cole, 1988), 207. This section of the chapter draws heavily on Wright's work.

2. Ibid., 212.

3. Ibid.

4. Ibid., 212–213.

5. This discussion is drawn from Beryl A. Radin, "A Landscape of Contradictions: American Federalism and Public Policy," in *Multiple Identities in a Single State: India Federalism in Comparative Perspective,* ed. Balveer Arora and Douglas Verney (Delhi: Konark Publishers, 1995).

6. See discussion in Wright, *Understanding Intergovernmental Relations,* 293. See also Theodore J. Lowi, "Four Systems of Policy, Politics, and Choice," *Public Administration Review* 32 (July–August 1972): 298–310; Paul E. Peterson, *City Limits* (Chicago: University of Chicago Press, 1981); and Samuel H. Beer, "The Modernization of American Federalism," *Publius* 3 (fall 1973): 49–96.

7. Wright, *Understanding Intergovernmental Relations,* 368.

8. Robert Pear, "U.S. Toughens Enforcement of Nursing Home Standards," *New York Times,* December 4, 2000, A21.

9. Wright, *Understanding Intergovernmental Relations,* 339.

10. See Peterson, *City Limits.*

11. David Price, "Policymaking in Congressional Committees: The Impact of 'Environmental' Factors," *American Political Science Review* 72 (1978): 548–574.

12. William T. Gormley Jr. and Cristina Boccuti, "HCFA and the States: Politics and Intergovernmental Leverage," *Journal of Health Politics, Policy, and Law* 26 (2001): 559.

13. Mark Yessian, "The Generalist Perspective in the HEW Bureaucracy: An Account from the Field," *Public Administration Review* 40 (March–April 1980).

14. James Q. Wilson, *Bureaucracy: What Government Agencies Do and Why They Do It* (New York: Basic Books, 1989), 91.

15. Martin A. Levin and Mary Bryna Sanger, *Making Government Work: How Entrepreneurial Executives Turn Bright Ideas into Real Results* (San Francisco: Jossey-Bass, 1994), 177.

16. Donna E. Shalala, *Public Administration Review* 58 (July–August 1998): 285.

17. Ibid.

18. Wright, *Understanding Intergovernmental Relations,* 83.

19. See Beryl A. Radin, "Intergovernmental Relationships and the Federal Performance Movement," *Publius: The Journal of Federalism* (winter 2000).

Accountability and the Politics Lens

RAYMOND WILSON thought that the political world of California had prepared him for almost anything. The size of the state, its mixture of ethnic groups and cultures, the presence of well-organized and articulate interest groups, and highly charged and partisan debates seemed to be good training for what he might expect in Washington.

Despite this California experience, he is shocked by what he is experiencing during the weeks between the announcement of his appointment as HHS secretary and the confirmation hearings. Phone calls and faxes seem never-ending from what appear to be hundreds of different interest groups with concerns about some part of the department's programs. Somehow people have found his home e-mail address and he is overwhelmed by the number of messages he receives every week. These contacts reinforce what he has already learned: interest groups can be found on every side of an issue. If he satisfies one group, he is likely to experience the rage of other groups.

Although he is focusing on the members of the Senate assigned to the two committees with jurisdiction over his confirmation, his contacts with members of Congress and their staffs are not limited to those two committees. Members and staff of the appropriations committees want to get their views known about the availability of resources for their "favorite" programs. Members even focus on specific grants to institutions and organizations in their districts. For example, he was dressing for a New Year's Eve party when he received an urgent call from a member of Congress from Colorado who was concerned about a grant to the University of Denver.

In addition, Wilson is in almost hourly contact with the members of the transition team about a range of issues. He knows that most of the individuals on the team are going to be placed in policy and political jobs in the White House and so he is likely to have to deal with them in the future. These individuals not only remind him about the campaign promises made by the president-elect, but they also give him a sense of the issues that will likely interest the White House in the future.

He realizes that the Washington political perspective is very broad. Politics permeates every set of actions. He reminds himself about the questions that he has identified soon after receiving the nomination.

- How much attention should the secretary give to the multiple actors involved in the department's operations? How should he sort out the roles of the internal bureaucracy, the interest groups, Congress, and the White House? How should the secretary think about the public, since so many of the department's programs directly touch citizens?
- Should the secretary attempt to have a direct role in choosing the political appointees who will be named to head the program units? What is the best strategy to ensure that the political team within the department generally shares a set of values and approaches?
- Who can the secretary trust? Should he rely only on the political appointees who will move into the department or can he trust the career public servants who are found within the various programs and offices?

THIS CHAPTER begins with the assumption that politics and administration are strongly entwined. It focuses on the role of interest groups and constituencies, congressional expectations and roles (including appointments, budget, and oversight), and the role of the White House (particularly OMB's role in the budget process, policy initiatives, the appointments process, and the impact of elections). All these demands require the HHS secretary to approach the job with skill and talent in juggling multiple demands.

For nearly a century, there have been players in and students of public administration who have viewed the work of the public sector as a set of tasks and responsibilities that could be separated from the world of politics. There were important reasons for reaching for this perspective (especially during the early years of the twentieth century, when political corruption was rampant in many American cities). According to James W. Fesler and Donald F. Kettl, "Establishing a neutral realm for administration, protected by civil service laws and governed by a drive for businesslike efficiency, would both dry up patronage resources of machines and leave policymaking organs of government as the proper realm for democratic politics."[1] But the belief in the politics/administration dichotomy had real limits.

The search for neutrality and clear delineation between the world of administration and the world of politics continues to preoccupy many in the public administration or public management field. This quest has taken many different forms, among them the functional separation of career public servants and political appointees, the differentiation between generalists and specialists, the balance between insiders and outsiders on staff, and rules that both prohibit and limit exchanges between the career bureaucracy and outside groups.

Few, however, would argue that it is possible to separate politics and administration when looking at the role of a cabinet secretary. Individuals who achieve the cabinet rank usually come in with a clear set of political contacts, political experience, and a policy agenda. Some of them have had experience as managers but mostly within the private rather than the public sector. Even those with public sector experience rarely have been tested in the environment of shared power and multiple masters that typifies the federal government reality.

Mark H. Moore has characterized individuals such as these as political managers and has suggested that the most effective managers are those who approach their job as entrepreneurial advocates. He notes that this approach "focuses on what a public manager needs to do to maximize the chance that his or her preferred policy will be authoritatively adopted and solidly backed."[2] Moore's depiction of the political manager tends to accentuate the areas of control and autonomy that make it possible for such an individual to devise tactics that mobilize support and neutralize opposition in order to achieve a policy agenda.

Although this proactive approach is both necessary and important, the world of politics often creates pressures and problems for a cabinet secretary that require a combination of proactive and reactive strategies. The American system of shared powers and the openness and permeability of the departments and agencies give a cabinet official much less autonomy and control than might be found in a parliamentary system, where legislative and executive functions are intertwined. Cabinet officials must be prepared for the unexpected—and the unexpected often comes from those who emphasize a political approach to issues and who operate outside of the department or organization with their own perspectives and agendas.

Three sets of political actors have the ability to make accountability demands that directly affect a cabinet official and his or her staff. These are interest groups, Congress, and the White House. Each of these sets of actors has its own method of expressing its political demands. Some are related to the structure of government, some to the electoral process, some to the relationships that flow from partisanship, and others to the dynamics of interest group politics.

DEALING WITH INTEREST GROUPS AND CONSTITUENCIES

The development of political associations is one of the characteristics of the American society that was described by the French observer Alexis de Tocqueville in the early part of the nineteenth century. He observed that "[i]n America the citizens who form the minority associate in order, first, to show their numerical strength and so to diminish the moral power of the majority; and, secondly, to stimulate competition and thus to discover those arguments that are most fitted to act upon the majority."[3] This predilection to develop organizations that represent specific interests has been an attribute of the American political system throughout its history. These organizations have come to be known as interest groups—specialized groups that are attentive to the details of policy making within the formal institutions of governance.

Because of shared agendas and perspectives, interest groups work closely with both congressional committees and executive branch entities to articulate demands, advocate for resources, and monitor the implementation of specific programs. These lobbying activities not only influence the decision making process but also serve an educational function, providing information to elected officials and other groups. When there are frequent shifts in elected officials, the interest groups provide an institutional memory, giving information about the success or failure of past efforts to elected officials.

This tripartite relationship (interest groups, congressional committees and staffs, and the career bureaucracy) has been called the "iron triangle," providing some mechanism for communication and stability in a highly fragmented political system.[4] As the interdependencies between program elements have become more obvious, they have resulted in what Hugh Heclo called "issue networks"— a web of largely autonomous participants with variable degrees of mutual commitment or dependence on each other.[5]

It is not surprising, given the proliferation of interest groups within U.S. society, that these groups differ in the way they relate to the agencies and issues that are of interest to them. James Q. Wilson has defined four different types of political environments that reflect different approaches by interest groups. The first is viewed as *client* politics, an environment in which a dominant interest group operates that enjoys most or all of the benefits of a program. The second is termed *entrepreneurial* politics, where costs of implementation are heavily concentrated on a few actors but the benefits are spread over many. In this situation, often a hostile interest group representing those who bear the cost of actions will be at play. The third is *interest group* politics, where rival interest groups operate who differ about the appropriate behavior of the agency. And the fourth is *majoritarian* politics, in which no interest group is continuously active and the agency behavior has both low costs and low benefits.[6] The interest groups that play a role in HHS are drawn from all four of these types.

John Kingdon has commented on the variety of interest group activity. He notes that "[s]ome of it affects the agenda; other activity affects the alternatives considered by policy makers. Some of it is positive, promoting new courses of government action; other activity is negative, seeking to block changes in public policy."[7] He also found that the role of interest groups shifts, depending on the issue at hand.

Interest groups vary dramatically in terms of their level of resources, their historical relationship with agencies, and the strategies they employ to articulate their positions and demands. Groups also differ in the way they influence the system. Some groups have created access to the decision-making system through campaign contributions; others (such as groups of elected officials) have influence because of their link to elections and partisan politics. James Q. Wilson has commented that these groups benefit from an increase in the number of points through which the system can be entered. Yet, he noted, although it has become easier to access government, greater access does not mean that it has become easier to alter government policy.[8]

William Browne has argued that interest groups in the United States have managed to accomplish four things.

> First, they've placed policy ideas in the context of mainstream American popular images . . . . Second, organized interests have long done comprehensive or even all-directional lobbying, and for a reason . . . . When organized interests aimed at targets in order to sell their marketable ideas, the targets were the public and the media, various public officials, and, of course, other interests . . . . Third, lobbyists have always sought strategically good issues and avoided bad ones . . . . Fourth, in a very complex way, the most successful of American interests have long fit their own environments. They've sought to be identified circumstantially as legitimate and credible policy players, to fit.[9]

The range of programs within HHS and the diverse modes of implementation of those programs have produced a thicket of interest groups usually attached to specific programs or specific agencies within the department. These interest groups illustrate each of the types described by Wilson; in some cases, however, the group's constituency combines types of groups and creates a variation on the Wilson themes. Interest groups differ in their ability to influence the system and thus vary in the kinds of accountability responses they evoke from an agency.

Perhaps more than in other situations, HHS interest groups can be viewed as representing those who actually provide the services that are funded by the federal government as well as those who advocate on behalf of citizens who would be served by the federal program. Organizations that represent providers of services speak in their own self-interest but their cooperation is essential if the federal dollars are to result in program implementation. In those cases, the relationship between the agency and the interest group is one of mutual dependence. In still other instances interest groups seek to speak on behalf of the general public—articulating positions that they argue are in the public interest, focusing on consumers of programs such as public health offerings.

The range of relationships HHS has with interest groups is illustrated by several organizations: the American Association of Retired Persons (AARP), the United Network for Organ Sharing (UNOS), organizations involved in welfare reform, Native American organizations, and the tobacco industry.

AARP

AARP is a nonprofit membership association that represents Americans who are more than fifty years of age.[10] The range of membership includes workers and retirees, individuals in their fifties who are still working and those over eighty living alone, people with comfortable standards of living and those struggling with minimal resources. AARP is the largest nonprofit organization dedicated to the interests of mature Americans.

Governed by a volunteer board of directors elected by delegates to the biennial conventions, the organization offers educational programs and activities that promote social welfare. All these efforts are undertaken to promote independence, dignity, and purpose for older Americans.

The lobbying efforts of the AARP are well known at both the state and federal levels, focused on a variety of issues that are needed to improve the lives of older Americans. That agenda is developed based on information from members and others through letters, legislative town hall meetings, surveys, and polls. Although the organization describes its public policy agenda as a "wish list," it operates within the constraints imposed by the federal budget and protects its status as a nonpartisan organization.

The Medicare program, administered by the CMS, is among the priority issues of the organization. As a strong supporter of the program, the AARP has sought to maintain and strengthen Medicare so that it will continue to provide high-quality, affordable health care coverage for current and future beneficiaries. It has emphasized the protection of Medicare's solvency and has attempted to address demographic shifts and delivery system changes in the health care marketplace.

The AARP has focused both on the relevant policy discussions in Congress and on the implementation efforts within the CMS. During the late 1990s it highlighted the implementation of the payment system within the CMS for the

Medicare+ Choice plans, accentuating the payment rates and safeguards involving quality of care and other consumer protections within contracts.

UNOS

The development of organ transplantation settings in the 1970s created a need for an organization that represented all U.S. transplant centers and other medical settings that were involved in the transplant process. In 1977 the United Network for Organ Sharing (UNOS) was created as a service to the more than ninety transplant centers across the country.[11] With the passage of the National Organ Transplant Act, the HHS secretary was authorized to establish a national Organ Procurement and Transplantation Network (OPTN) in the private sector. The OPTN is responsible for establishing membership criteria and medical criteria for organ allocation and operates a twenty-four-hour computer system for listing patients awaiting transplants and matching donated organs with those patients. It also provides twenty-four-hour organ placement assistance and works actively to increase the organ supply.

In 1986 UNOS was awarded the federal contract to establish and operate the OPTN. As a result, it not only serves to articulate the needs of the transplantation network but also to determine the policies and criteria that govern the activity. The organization itself is structured to represent eleven regions, and its board includes transplant surgeons or physicians, patients, donors, and family members. The UNOS computer-matching system generates a priority ranking of patients in specific geographical areas. The federal law requires that organs be allocated to patients based on medical criteria, not social criteria, or economic status.

Over the years UNOS has worked closely with the Office of Special Programs in HRSA. In effect, the federal agency is dependent on UNOS to implement the program. In 1998 HHS issued regulations that attempted to provide greater equity in the organ transplantation system, moving toward a more national rather than regional allocation of organs. UNOS did not agree with these proposed regulations and was able to use its close relationship with members of Congress to block their implementation. However, in 2000, HHS was able to separate some of the functions that it had contracted to UNOS and, while retaining UNOS's administration of the network, gave another nonprofit group responsibility for the scientific registry of transplant recipients.

Organizations Involved in Welfare Reform

For more than twenty-five years, attempts to modify the existing welfare system have preoccupied many interest groups within the United States. The passage of the Personal Responsibility and Work Opportunity Reconciliation (PRWOR) Act of 1996 provided a window to explicate this array of interest group participants, indicating the differences among those who attempted to influence the changes. Unlike some of the other examples in this discussion, welfare reform interest group activity illustrates major differences in values, perspectives, and approaches of these actors.

One can cluster these groups into four categories. The first involves representatives of state and local governments. The second includes associations of people who seek to speak for specific groups affected by the proposed changes. The third involves individuals who were providers of existing services and are likely to be affected by proposed modifications. And the fourth group involves organizations that had conducted research on the effectiveness of existing programs and attempted to analyze anticipated impacts of proposed changes.[12]

State and Local Governments. For many years, the National Governors' Association (NGA) and spokespeople for individual states sought to make changes in the welfare system. Part of their concern was generated by the large expenditure of state funds required by the program (approximately 50 percent of the cost of welfare was paid by the federal government; the remainder was paid by the states or, depending on the location, by local governments). As it advocated for changes in the system, the NGA also argued that the existing Aid to Families With Dependent Children (AFDC) program was not effective, particularly because it did not provide incentives for recipients to move out of welfare dependency. The bottom line for the NGA was to maximize the discretion of individual states to deal with these issues and minimize the federal requirements for the program. Movement to a block grant program was the preferred approach.

Although the NGA was the major general purpose government player in the policy discussion, representatives of local government were also involved. Groups such as the National League of Cities expressed concern about the impact of changes in the system. Some representatives of local government were concerned that state governments (governors and state legislatures) would minimize state responsibility for needy populations and pass the responsibility to local governments without providing them with adequate resources to meet these problems. Similar concerns were also voiced by representatives of American Indian tribes.

Advocates for Welfare Recipients. This category of interest groups was extremely varied. It included individuals who sought to speak for specific groups (such as children, women, and families) and highlighted the impact of proposed changes on those specific populations. Each of these interest groups developed its argument based on its assessment of the effectiveness of existing programs, its view of the short-term versus the long-term impact on individual recipients, and its value orientation. This cluster included social change advocates (such as the Childrens' Defense Fund, the Center for Law and Social Policy, the Center on Budget and Policy Priorities, individuals from various women's organizations, and representatives of community action programs).[13] Other players included faith-based groups, individuals concerned about fatherhood and families, and more conservative organizations such as the American Enterprise Institute.

Providers. Representatives of those who provided both existing and proposed services to welfare recipients were also important interest group players in the policy debate. Although some of these organizations represented public sector providers (often at the state level) and were formally responsible to general purpose elected officials, their perspective was that of a specialist and revolved around professional concerns. These groups included organizations such as the American Public Human Services Association and the National Child Support Enforcement Association.

Researchers. Because much of the policy debate over welfare involved different perspectives on the relative success or failure of existing programs, several research organizations were involved in the process. Although these groups are not traditional interest groups, they did play an important role in the process of assessing the impact of proposals. This cluster included the Manpower Development Research Corporation and the Urban Institute.

Native American Organizations

The relationship between the programs and staff of the Indian Health Service and organizations that represent Indian people has always been an unusual one. Based on a special government-to-government relationship that flows from treaties between Indian nations and the U.S. government, for more than a century the IHS has attempted to work in partnership with American Indians and Alaska Natives to develop and manage programs to meet their health needs. The passage of the Indian Self-Determination Act and executive orders further accentuated the commitment to involve tribes, Indian organizations, and Indian people in the process.

In 1995 an Indian Health Design Team was convened that included twenty-two representatives of Indian tribes and communities and several other stakeholders. This group issued a report in which it sought to avoid being overtaken by forces that were responding to priorities different from those of Indian people. It also responded to the reality that more tribes were taking over the delivery of health care through self-determination contracts and self-governance compacts. The effort was described as the first time that Indian people have guided the process to design a health care system that works best for them.

The report received feedback from a range of tribal governments, from nonprofit health boards throughout the country, through national Indian organizations such as the National Indian Health Board and the National Indian Council on Aging, and from IHS employees, many of whom are also Native Americans.

These groups (and others) also act as the voice for the Indian people during congressional deliberations, especially those involving the appropriations process. Over several years, increases were made in the budget amounts requested by the White House for IHS because of the lobbying efforts of the Indian community.

During the 1990s, efforts organized by HHS such as the Indian Health Design Team have resulted in a commitment to establish a close relationship between the IHS and the groups that articulate the interests of the Indian people. The concept of partnership is used frequently to describe what is almost a symbiotic relationship between these groups and the agency. It is difficult to establish clear boundary lines between the two.

The Tobacco Industry

For many years the tobacco industry was visible and active in federal policies involving agriculture. A. Lee Fritschler described the tobacco interest group community as including the paid representatives of tobacco growers, marketing organizations, and cigarette manufacturers.[14] This cluster of actors focused on the appropriations and substantive legislative committees in each house of Congress as well as on officials within the U.S. Department of Agriculture involved with various tobacco programs.

It was not until 1954 with the release of research studies that dealt with smokers and nonsmokers that the tobacco interest group cluster began to focus on public health issues and, as a result, on the programs of the U.S. Public Health Service. Responding to data that seemed to the public health community to clearly indicate that smoking causes lung cancer, the tobacco community organized itself to focus on the emerging health research findings. The Tobacco Industry Research Committee (TIRC) was formed jointly by U.S. tobacco manufacturers, growers, and warehousemen in 1954 as the primary institution that would help the industry present an alternative answer to the question, is there a relationship between smoking and health? The public announcement of the creation of the TIRC noted that the group was being formed in response to scientific reports suggesting a link between smoking and lung cancer and that the purpose of the TIRC was to fund independent scientific research to determine whether these reports were true. In 1964 the organization was renamed the Council for Tobacco Research—USA (CTR).

From 1954 to 1980 the organization awarded 744 grants totaling $64 million to 413 scientists at 258 hospitals, laboratories, research organizations, and medical schools. According to Fritschler, 1,882 reports were published during that period acknowledging support from the TIRC/CTR.[15] There has been considerable dispute over the years about the pressure that was placed on those who received research grants to come up with findings that minimized the health risks of tobacco.

In 1958 a lobbying public relations group was formed to "contain the possible adverse political effects of the health studies."[16] Called the Tobacco Institute, the organization employed classic public relations techniques to attempt to minimize the impact of a growing concern about the effects of tobacco. By 1964 the release of the surgeon general's report on smoking and health stimulated direct attention to the decision-making processes within HEW/HHS. Although the report acknowledged that the research had not thus far established the precise role of smoking in causing chronic disease, it did warn that "[c]igarette smoking is a health hazard of sufficient importance in the United States to warrant appropriate remedial action." In 1965 legislation was enacted that required each pack of cigarettes to contain a label warning of the negative health effects of smoking.

The strategy that was adopted by the tobacco organizations highlighted the uncertainty about the public health research findings. At the same time, the industry's arguments emphasized the economic effects of regulating the tobacco industry in those states (largely in the South) that were dependent on tobacco for jobs, using classic political influencing means to support their positions. Some observers saw the CTR as not really a research enterprise but, rather, a political and legal shield for the industry.[17]

During the 1970s the Federal Trade Commission (FTC) was the center of attempts to regulate the tobacco industry. But by the mid-1990s efforts by the FDA to classify tobacco as an addictive substance further stimulated activity by the tobacco industry. It sharpened its arguments to challenge the FDA's authority to regulate tobacco; it also waged a high-profile campaign against the commissioner of the FDA, David Kessler, and highlighting what they saw as the political consequences of moving to a regulatory posture.[18]

Disclosure of further research findings linking tobacco and health problems and a concerted effort by groups such as the American Cancer Society, the American Heart Association, and Smoke Free Kids changed the environment in which the tobacco industry operated. FDA investigators were able to identify researchers who had been employees of or were funded by the industry and were able to cast doubt on the integrity of the work sponsored by the CTR. Litigation increased against the industry with cases brought by individuals whose health problems were attributable to smoking. And several states began to focus on the monetary costs of treating individuals who were addicted to tobacco. The industry was able to challenge the regulations that were issued by the FDA, and the U.S. Supreme Court ruled that the FDA had exceeded its authority. In 1998 a settlement was reached between the industry and the attorney generals from forty-six states. Although that agreement called for the elimination of the CTR as well as the Tobacco Institute, the industry continued to make its case against the linking of tobacco and health.

As the example of the tobacco groups indicates, over time interest groups may experience changes in their ability to influence decision makers. Elections, the press, and crises may shift the way the society perceives an issue. Yet, at the same time, agencies are dependent on the interest groups not only for political support but for implementation of programs.

CONGRESSIONAL EXPECTATIONS AND ROLES

The American system of shared powers has created a role for the legislative branch in administrative matters that is quite unlike that found in most other countries. Whether or not this role is perceived to be counterproductive to achieving the efficiency of decision-making processes, the role of Congress has to be taken seriously in the processes of managing cabinet departments.[19]

Political institutions in the United States, wherever they are found and whatever they are called, are constructed to minimize or, if possible, avoid the exertion of concentrated power. Power and authority are separated and shared across all aspects of the political landscape. This occurs horizontally through the delineation of separate institutions charged with executive, legislative, and judicial functions as well as vertically through the assumption of shared or separate powers between the national, state, and sometimes local levels of government. The principle of fragmentation is carried on within institutions (for example, bicameral legislatures and separation of authorizing and appropriations functions within the legislative branch) as well as across most levels of government (for example, shared powers between a state governor and a state legislature or between a city mayor and a city council). Divided government, with the executive branch represented by one political party and the legislative branch (in at least one of the bicameral bodies) represented by another party, is very often a reality in Washington and in many states. Unlike many other countries, the United States did not begin with the reality of a strong national government. Rather, the American state developed largely from a bottom-up distribution of power.

As a result, unlike a parliamentary system, there is no institutional actor with authority to look at the government as a whole. Except in emergency situations such as wartime, the American system would not permit the creation of a national planning commission such as that in many countries or even a body charged with allocating funds within program areas to the separate states. The political process, with its vagaries, determines the allocation pattern.[20]

The internal structure of Congress mirrors the larger fragmentation of political power. The narrow jurisdictions of congressional committees and subcommittees not only reflect the organizational structure of the federal bureaucracy but also separate the legislative functions of appropriating funds from authorizing programs.[21] This fragmentation often results in conflict between the congressional units; Allen Schick has noted that this conflict has existed since the appropriations committees were established during the Civil War era.[22] In addition, Congress has a role in making decisions involving functions that might be viewed as administrative prerogatives (such as appointments, organizational structure, and other management functions).

James Q. Wilson has focused on both the limits and the opportunities related to congressional control of the bureaucracy, reflecting the complexity of the shared-power system. He notes that although Congress can determine the number of employees an agency will have, it has limited ability to determine who those employees will be. Similarly, Congress can decide how much money an agency might spend on personnel, but it cannot determine the pay of individual staffers. Congress can fix the total expenditures of an agency and the amount that can be spent on particular projects, but it often leaves the specific changes in expenditures to a formula approach.[23] Wilson also argues that the extent and form of legislative control involving a particular program or agency stems from what he calls "a subtle and complex interplay between tasks and environment."[24]

Although a cabinet secretary cannot ignore any of the concerns that are expressed by members of Congress about program implementation, there are three formal processes within Congress that are especially important: confirmation of appointees, approval of the budget, and the authorizing/oversight role. Bernard Rosen has noted that the involvement of Congress comes in many different forms; some emerge from problems that are raised by constituents and others from regularly scheduled processes, particularly the budget process.[25] In reality, the budget process is the lifeblood of agencies, and the executive branch cannot ignore or easily finesse its strictures.

Confirmation of Appointees

Beyond the requirement for Senate confirmation of members of the cabinet, some subcabinet officials also require Senate approval—the advise and consent process. These individuals—nominated by the president—make up the first tier of staff for any administration. Members of Congress have the ability not only to withhold approval of these individuals but, more important, to use the hearings attached to the confirmation process to communicate their expectations about the job in question. Senate committees that have responsibilities for confirming both cabinet and subcabinet officials have been encouraged to focus on leadership and management skills that might be appropriate for running federal agencies.[26]

Within HHS eighteen officials require Senate confirmation. Four of the positions these officials will hold have been viewed as particularly important by John H. Trattner, author of *The 2000 Prune Book*.[27] These include the positions of commissioner of the Food and Drug Administration, director of the

National Institutes of Health, administrator of the Centers for Medicare and Medicaid, and assistant secretary for Children and Families. The confirmation process in each of these positions varies; the FDA position (according to a former commissioner) "will always get a great deal of scrutiny, no matter what administration or Congress you're talking about."[28] The NIH director, by contrast, can use the confirmation process to create and sustain support for research. The size and scope of the CMS position and activities (particularly the extensive dependence on care providers) push members of Congress to demand action from that appointee.[29] And the volatility and controversy surrounding a great number of programs within the Administration for Children and Families portfolio also establish an opening for members of Congress to raise issues during the confirmation process.

Although it is rare for Congress to turn down HHS subcabinet appointments (or, for that matter, the cabinet position), the confirmation does provide an opportunity for the relevant committees to raise issues and provide signals to the appointees about the areas that are likely to be the subject of budget, authorizing, and oversight scrutiny. In some cases, such as the battles over the confirmation of the surgeon general, members of Congress have used the confirmation process as a vehicle to debate specific policy approaches.

The Budget Process

As Allen Schick has observed, "In budgeting . . . there is conflict and resolution. Politics and process have a dual role in igniting conflict and in prodding the protagonists to set aside their differences."[30] The results of the budget process, writes Schick, "is much more than a matter of dollars."

> It finances federal programs and agencies and is a vital means of establishing and pursuing national priorities. In a fundamental sense, the federal government is what it spends. Through the budget, the government assists millions of families in meeting basic expenses and provides a financial safety net for the sick, elderly, and other dependent persons. The budget invests in the country's future by paying for roads and other physical assets, as well as for education and other human improvements.[31]

Bernard Rosen has noted that the regularity of the appropriations process and the system used to make appropriations are key. He suggests that this process becomes the focal point for interactions between agencies and Congress:

> Despite the fact that limited time and the size and complexity of the budgets make it impossible for these [appropriations committees and subcommittees] to give careful consideration to all major problems for which funds are requested, various sources of information help focus their attention on important problem areas. Subcommittee staffs, through periodic or occasional contacts

with agency officials during the year, have opportunities to become informed about major policy and program developments that have implications for current or future expenditures.[32]

The relative predictability and regularity of the budget process give the development of a budget a special status within the often turbulent and unpredictable Washington environment. Thus a cabinet secretary usually pays special attention to the details of the appropriations process. Although other aspects of the budget process are important (for example, the bargaining between agencies within departments and their secretaries as well as the exchange between departments and the White House via OMB), in recent decades the role of Congress in budgeting has become especially important. Since the enactment of the 1974 Congressional Budget and Impoundment Control Act establishing the congressional budget process, Congress has established its own budgetary independence.[33] From 1974 to the end of the 1990s this posture was reinforced by two developments—the reality of divided government and the concern about the budget deficit.

In addition, some attempt has been made to use the reports and analyses performed by the General Accounting Office during the budget process. The GAO is the investigative arm of Congress. According to its self-definition it exists to support Congress in meeting its constitutional responsibilities and to help improve the performance and accountability of the federal government for the American people. The GAO examines the use of public funds, evaluates federal programs and activities, and provides analyses, options, recommendations, and other assistance to help Congress make effective oversight, policy, and funding decisions through financial audits, program reviews and evaluations, analyses, legal opinions, investigations, and other services.

The congressional players in the budget process include the House and Senate appropriations committees and subcommittees as well as the House and Senate budget committees. The details of the specific allocations are established by the appropriations units, whereas the ground rules for budget totals and functional allocations are established by the budget committees. Although the budget committees do play an important role, from the perspective of a cabinet department, the specific decisions of the appropriations units are crucial.

Unlike the situation for some other cabinet-level departments, the appropriations authority for HHS is dispersed among several subcommittees in both the House and the Senate. Three separate appropriations subcommittees in each of the chambers have authority over parts of the HHS budget. As a result, although the department's budget is prepared as a whole, it is not evaluated by the congressional players in its entirety. The subunits within the department each have hearings before the appropriations subcommittees, responding to specific questions and concerns about their programs and policies. The FDA budget is presented to subcommittees of the appropriations committee that largely deal with the Department of Agriculture, while the Indian Health Service budget is presented to the subcommittees that also deal with the Department of Interior. The remainder of the HHS budget is presented to the subcommittees that deal with labor, education, human services, and health. Congress can also focus on units within units; for example, the budget of the National Cancer Institute is described as a bypass budget. Congress has stipulated that the NCI director should present a budget to Congress at the same time that it is submitted to both the HHS secretary and the NIH director.

In addition, as if the process were not complicated enough, the HHS budget items take two different forms. One chunk of the budget is called *entitlements or mandatory programs,* based on legal provisions that obligate the federal government to make payments to eligible recipients. Entitlement authority may be funded in either an annual or permanent appropriation. Most of the CMS budget authority takes the entitlement form, as do programs inside of the ACF, particularly the welfare reform program and several other programs involving children. The second part of the budget, termed *discretionary* spending, is based on budget authority (other than appropriated entitlements) that takes the form of annual appropriations. Discretionary spending items tend to elicit more attention during the appropriations subcommittee hearings.

Each of the HHS program units presents its budget to the appropriate appropriations committee following an overall presentation by the secretary (usually limited to the House and Senate subcommittees that have authority over most of the programs). These hearings vary tremendously in their style and dynamics, often reflecting the level of controversy involving the program. In a few instances, Congress is a champion of an agency or program, and members actually vie with one another to find ways to add to the administration's budget request. Because many HHS programs deal with health issues and matters of life and death, those programs (especially the research efforts) are able to generate considerable support within Congress.

The NIH budget process is unlike any other part of the appropriations process, both in the way the agency makes its presentation to the subcommittees and—perhaps more important—in the way members treat the agency. As John Trattner characterized it, "The Congress has been turned on by the NIH for years. Legislators of both parties . . . have since the 1960s been generous with NIH budgets, consistently giving the agency more than it requested even in times of severe federal deficit and fierce battles for available funds."[34] The reality of biomedical research means that NIH presents its accomplishments to Congress not as achievements during any one specific year or focused on a specific allocation but as efforts over many years and across subunits within the NIH. For the world of research, unanticipated results are often more useful than those contained in research protocols.

During much of the 1990s, members of Congress across both political parties were largely willing to provide the NIH with funds with minimal requirements (stipulation of specifics is called earmarking) for specific units or specific diseases, departing from the traditional way of adding funds to administration requests. A large percentage of the NIH budget (for example, approximately 60 percent of the funds in fiscal year 1995) was designated as basic research, which frequently cut across subunits within the agency and contributed to the pursuit of understanding a collection of diseases. As the director of the NIH put it, "The clinical triumphs that we enjoy this year were possible only because we had invested successfully in many fields of basic science—bacteriology, virology, enzymology, chemistry and others."[35] The arguments that were advanced during appropriations committee hearings emphasized the bipartisan support for these types of programs.

In other program areas, however, members of Congress use the appropriations process to target specific issues. During the late 1990s, members of the Congressional Black Caucus raised issues during the appropriations process about the level of funds that were being spent to deal with HIV and AIDS issues among African American citizens. AIDS deaths among African Americans are nearly ten times those of whites.[36] In addition, the caucus expressed concern about what it viewed as inadequate attention to the problems of African Americans within the NIH and HRSA. Efforts were also developed to encourage nonprofit and indigenous organizations serving African Americans to get involved in the provision of comprehensive outpatient HIV primary care services. When $50 million was earmarked in the 2000 and 2001 budgets for prevention and treatment of individuals with HIV/AIDS in minority communities, Congress required that the department submit an operating plan for the use of those funds to both the House and Senate appropriations committees.

Some years earlier, advocates of women's issues had also put pressure on the NIH through the appropriations process to pay more attention to diseases of women and to focus on differences between men and women during clinical trials. Both of these concerns resulted in the creation of specialized offices within the Office of the Director of the NIH to focus on these populations.

Congress has also used a variant on the legislative veto to limit the discretion of the HHS agencies. The legislative veto is a controversial practice in which Congress gives itself the ability to review the administrative regulations issued by an agency. Although the Supreme Court drastically limited the practice, it continues to exist in some programs. In the fiscal year 2000 budget, HRSA was told that before it could issue regulations related to the Organ Transplant program, it had to give Congress forty-two days to review those regulations. The previous year, HRSA was told that its final regulations could not become effective for one year. Both of these actions provided Congress with the ability to stop the agency from acting to change the program in a direction that some members of Congress opposed.

The appropriations process for some of the HHS programs can be character-ized as highly volatile and conflict-laden. Often these conflicts are embedded in very different partisan perspectives on programs, particularly in environments of divided government. During the mid-1990s, after gaining control of both the House and the Senate, the Republicans were able to use studies and reports is-sued by the GAO during the appropriations hearings and afterward to raise seri-ous questions about programs. In the case of the Head Start program, for exam-ple, a series of GAO reports were cited by Republicans on one of the House appropriations subcommittees to question the effectiveness of the federal expen-ditures for that program. The GAO reports not only helped the majority side of the subcommittee staff draft questions to the ACF assistant secretary but also were used to generate follow-up questions to be answered by the assistant secre-tary. The answers to those questions were developed by the agency for the sub-committee.

But for other programs, support for federal expenditures transcended parti-san differences because the programs were important for constituents. Several programs within HRSA have generated significant support from Republicans because they provide essential services to their constituents. Both the commu-nity health centers and the rural health programs were viewed as important by Republican members of Congress representing small towns or rural areas. If ei-ther of those programs evaporated or were significantly cut, there would be no health services at all in those districts. Individual members sometimes supported these programs despite opposition to them within the Republican Party leader-ship.

Since 1997 Congress also had available to it the information developed by agencies under the requirements of the Government Performance and Results Act (GPRA). The GPRA requirements for development of annual performance plans and annual performance reports are structured to be data elements attached to the budget submission. Many assumptions embedded in GPRA have estab-lished quite difficult pathways to implementation. First, it assumes that a single piece of information will be able to meet the complex decision-making needs of both the executive and legislative branches. Second, the focus on outcome per-formance measures (and the avoidance of process and output measures) deni-grates the role of the federal government in many program areas. Third, it as-sumes that it is possible to directly link planning, management, and budgeting processes through performance information. Fourth, it assumes that it is possible to avoid partisan political conflicts and the differences in policy constructs be-tween programs (programs that range from efforts that are delivered directly by the federal government to those that are hands-off block grants to others, partic-ularly state and local governments).[37] Although in a few instances congressional decisions regarding HHS budget allocations may have been affected by the

GPRA submissions, for the most part the GPRA data were used by Congress only to support pre-existing positions on specific programs.

The Oversight Process

The range of congressional committees and subcommittees charged with the authorizing process (that is, the creation of new laws or changes in existing laws) provides the setting for oversight for federal agencies. This authority was defined in the Legislative Reorganization Act of 1946.

> To assist the Congress in appraising the administration of the laws and in development of such amendments or related legislation as it may deem necessary, each standing committee of the Senate and the House shall exercise continuous watchfulness of the execution by the administrative agencies concerned of any laws, the subject matter of which is within the jurisdiction of such committee; and, for that purpose, shall study all pertinent reports and data submitted to the Congress by the agencies in the executive branch of the Government.[38]

Although oversight hearings are the most public form of oversight, other techniques are also used by members of Congress and their staffs. Joel Aberbach has compiled a list of these techniques. He found that the two bodies of Congress differ in their use of these techniques, although both houses use staff communication extensively. These techniques include:

- Staff communication
- Member communication
- Oversight hearings
- Program reauthorization hearings
- Amendment hearings
- Review of casework
- Staff investigations and field studies
- Analysis of proposed regulations
- Agency reports
- Congressional support agency program evaluations
- Agency program evaluations
- "Outsiders" program evaluations
- Committee staff program evaluations
- Legislative veto[39]

Overall, according to Aberbach, "congressional committees are quite capable of reaching and sustaining high levels of oversight activity. The design of American institutions and the concomitant incentives of those in Congress make this possible."[40] He also notes that the structure of the U.S. government actually encourages bureaucrats to "cut deals with congressmen who can protect their agencies from central executive control, to pursue the interests of clienteles who can help to protect their programs, and to act as advocates for interests inadequately represented through the ostensible channels of political representation." [41]

Since the passage of the Inspector General Act in 1978, Congress has also had available the studies of the inspector generals appointed to each of the cabinet departments to provide information both to the department secretary as well as to Congress. The inspector generals in departments were created to consolidate and organize the monitoring and investigative functions within agencies. They had broad access to information that they would analyze and report to both executive branch and legislative actors. Burdett Loomis's study of the House politicians elected in the 1970s described the way that Rep. Henry Waxman, Democrat from California, was able to elicit testimony from the HHS inspector general to the House Health and Environment Subcommittee. Loomis noted that

> Waxman demonstrates the potential that a well-staffed subcommittee offers an activist chair. Not only can he promote a pet project, as with his heroin proposal [to provide compassionate use as a pain reliever for the terminally ill], but he can push legislation to fruition through obtaining publicity (orphan drugs), tack on a program to a budget reconciliation bill (maternity benefits), and seek long-term political solutions to intractable policy problems . . . . If Waxman does not always emerge victorious—and he surely doesn't—he always comes to play, and a key subcommittee gives him lots of leeway to find a way to win. [42]

One of the most controversial issues in the 106th Congress dealt with the use of stem cells for research. These cells are those that have been derived from nonliving fetuses or living embryos and are used in research into health problems such as diabetes and heart disease. Congress had enacted legislation earlier that banned the use of cells drawn from nonliving fetuses or living embryos. In 1999 a legal opinion within HHS argued that stem cells are not embryos and that use of stem cells derived with the use of nonfederal funds was legitimate. [43] In 2000 legislation was introduced in the Senate to amend the Public Health Service Act to provide for research with respect to human embryonic stem cells. The legislation limited such research only to those stem cells derived from embryos that have been donated from in-vitro fertilization clinics with the written informed consent of the donors and that would otherwise be discarded. The bill was referred to the Senate Health, Education, Labor, and Pensions Committee, which held hearings on the measure. However, the House took no action during that year and the legislation resurfaced within the executive branch during the George W. Bush administration.

At times the members of Congress play a more open oversight role by creating special venues to examine a program. The National Bipartisan Commission on the Future of Medicare was created by Congress in the Balanced Budget Act of

1997. Under that act, the commission was given the job of examining the Medicare program and making recommendations to strengthen and improve it in time for the retirement of the baby boomers (those persons born between 1946 and 1964). The commission was charged with issuing a report to Congress and the administration by March 1, 1999. Sen. John Breaux, D-La., and Rep. Bill Thomas, R-Calif., jointly chaired the commission.

The commission was created because a future financial crisis was anticipated for Medicare when, in the year 2010, 77 million baby boomers will begin to enter Medicare and dramatically increase the demand for its services. At the same time, the number of workers per retiree will fall significantly. This commission was charged with finding real solutions for these very real financial threats.

The membership of the commission was designed so that no single political party had control. Furthermore, Congress stipulated that any recommendations made by the commission must have more than a simple majority to ensure bipartisan outcomes that represent people, not politics. Despite the seriousness with which this commission operated, it was not able to come to an agreement when its report was due.

Although congressional committees and subcommittees are very protective of their jurisdiction and authority, there are times when several units do support one another. In late 1999 and early 2000, there were disclosures that the CDC had not expended funds that had been appropriated by Congress for hantavirus, a pathogen that is related to what is called chronic fatigue syndrome, and had diverted the funds to other diseases and had sent misleading spending reports to the legislative branch. The disclosure stimulated criticism in Congress in the House and Senate appropriations committees, the House Government Reform Committee, and the House Commerce Committee. The criticism not only focused on this program area but questioned the veracity of the information that the CDC presented to the congressional committees. The response by HHS to this problem was to require that all financial decisions from the unit within the CDC involved in this issue be approved by senior financial officers at both the CDC and in the department.[44]

Like interest groups, congressional processes and venues create many different types of expectations for a cabinet secretary. In addition, elections and shifts in leadership in congressional committees modify those expectations. Although Congress is clearly affected by partisan politics, the closer that one gets to specific programs, the less that partisanship helps to explain congressional behavior.

POLITICS AND THE WHITE HOUSE

Because the selection of cabinet officials is viewed as one of the most important decisions made by a president, the popular press tends to view the relationship between a cabinet secretary and the White House as a relatively simple and always close tie. This view is reinforced by the language used to describe cabinet departments—that is, they are a part of the executive branch of government. This imagery not only flies in the face of the reality of shared power with the other two branches of government but it also masks the reality of the complexity of the contemporary White House and the Executive Office of the President.

Rufus Miles noted this tendency in his depiction of HHS in the 1970s: "The White House staff and the Office of Management and Budget constantly have their fingers in many of his [the Secretary's] pies, and on selected issues—not necessarily the biggest issues—the President brings his own special perspective and style to bear."[45] Fesler and Kettl describe the White House staff as "now so large, multitiered, and specialized that it itself is hard to coordinate . . . . Infighting among staff members to gain the president's ear has plagued every modern president."[46]

There are several aspects of internal executive branch politics that are particularly important for an HHS secretary to understand. These involve relationships around the budget process and OMB, specific White House initiatives, the appointment process, and efforts focused on electoral politics. [47]

The Budget Process and OMB

The budget that becomes the basis for the congressional appropriations process emerges from a highly stylized and protracted process involving the Executive Office of the President and cabinet departments. Fesler and Kettl described the power of OMB: "At the heart of its power is its function of annually reviewing all agencies' proposed expenditures in order to draft the government's budget for the president's review and transmittal to Congress."[48] This review process involves both White House political appointees as well as a sizable number of career OMB officials who exert a high level of institutional discretion.

One study of the role of these career officials up to 1980 found that on five measures of discretion, career staff in OMB came out high in regard to "the degree of supervision, degree of self-initiated information gathering, degree of discretion regarding clearance of testimony and legislative guidance to agency personnel, and discretion in determining small-dollar pricing issues."[49] Although the extent of discretion has varied over the years, depending on the expectations of a president and a president's staff, the OMB budget examiners have continued to play important roles in crafting budgets through their day-to-day dealings with department and agency-level staff.

The bottom-up budget creation process within OMB means that individual budget examiners have significant discretion and have sometimes advised their career and political supervisors to move in directions that are quite different from those proposed by an agency and a department. Over the years, there has been fairly consistent skepticism within OMB about several programs. For example, department requests for funds for the Health Professions Program in HRSA and for the programs of the Indian Health Service have been consistently cut by OMB. The department's requests have often been restored in Congress.

The department's proposed budget is submitted to OMB in September. The revisions to this proposed budget for a department are usually returned to the cabinet organization over the Thanksgiving weekend. At that point, department officials can appeal changes in their proposals to the OMB director. Eventually the cabinet secretary usually is able to make a personal appeal to the president for changes in the budget that would be submitted to Congress in January for the State of the Union address.

Over the years, the budget appeal process has been an important venue for an HHS secretary to raise policy issues. Although cuts are frequently recommended by OMB, many times the secretary has been successful in appealing them to the OMB director or to the president. During the Clinton administration, budget conflict rarely occurred within HHS, and a unified position was submitted to OMB. Instead of battling inside the department, the battle was moved to the Executive Office of the President.

Specific White House Initiatives

Whether as a result of campaign promises, political calculations, or crisis or emergent issues, the White House staff frequently plays an important role in crafting and strategizing specific policy initiatives. At times these efforts emerge from specific offices (such as the Domestic Policy Council or the Office of Policy Development) or come from other parts of the White House establishment. Over the years, offices such as the Office of Science and Technology Policy, the Office of National Drug Control Policy, and Vice President Gore's National Performance Review have played an important role in a specific administration.

The range and volatility of HHS issues make it inevitable that any White House is likely to express interest in policy areas that are within the HHS portfolio. These interests reflect calculations related to ideology, election strategies, and political advantage. Examples from the past decade that illustrate the White House involvement include health care reform, child care, needle exchange, the National Performance Review, and Y2K.

Health Care Reform. The massive effort that was orchestrated out of the White House in the first years of the Clinton administration was an attempt to reform the health care system. Led by First Lady Hillary Rodham Clinton, the President's Task Force on Health Care Reform was the latest in an array of efforts over the years to find a way to rationalize the nation's health care system, responding to issues of access, quality, and cost.[50] Although the programs and issues that were at the heart of the task force's work involved major elements in the

HHS policy and program portfolio, the department's involvement in the process was largely limited to its loan to the White House of health policy staff experts. Some observers of the process believed that more extensive involvement of HHS staff who were closer to the programs and relevant constituency groups would have led to a policy design that would have achieved public and congressional support. Instead, the proposal that emerged was subject to intense political and public criticism and died.

Child Care Programs. During the Clinton administration, federal funding for child care more than doubled, helping parents pay for the care of about 1.5 million children. Although the White House exhibited strong interest in this issue (much of it stimulated by First Lady Hillary Rodham Clinton's concerns), the mobilization of support for this program was a collaborative effort involving HHS officials in the Administration for Children and Families as well as White House staff assigned to work on the policy. It resulted in a bipartisan agreement with Congress to increase the funds available for child care through the Child Care and Development Block Grant.

Needle Exchange. Although the Office of National Drug Control Policy (ONDCP) involved representatives from a range of affected federal programs in its operations, there were times when the perspective of this office did not mesh with the concerns of HHS. A rather dramatic clash in perspectives was found in the debate over the administration's policy on needle exchange programs for drug users. Research that was supported and analyzed within the public health agencies in HHS indicated that programs for the exchange of used needles for new needles were able to reduce the incidence of HIV in that population. However, the staff in the ONDCP believed that providing needles for drug users would encourage drug use. That position prevailed in the Clinton administration until a compromise position was eventually crafted to give the secretary of HHS the authority to fund programs that can show that they are effective in reducing the transmission of HIV and do not increase drug abuse.

The National Performance Review. The National Performance Review (renamed the National Partnership for Reinventing Government) asked all cabinet members to create Reinvention Teams to lead transformations at their departments, and Reinvention Laboratories, to begin experimenting with new ways of doing business. The internal process within HHS began in September 1993; it operated out of the Office of the Deputy Secretary and was managed by a senior career staffer. It was named the Secretary's Continuous Improvement Program and involved more than 300 HHS employees working in six work groups. These groups were established to respond to "the more than 3,000 ideas which have been submitted to the Secretary, and to the recommendations from the Vice President's National Performance Review." The employee suggestions received by the effort emphasized leadership and management, program operations changes, customer services, and personnel management. Several principles were a part of the Continuous Improvement Program design: that it should complement, not duplicate, the health care and welfare reform efforts; that employee, customer, and partner participation should be recognized as critical; and that the design should be built on the secretary's three themes (fostering independence, prevention, and improving customer service). Career staffers chaired all six work groups. The advisory group for the effort met every week and the steering committee was convened once a month. The common thread in all the work groups was described as decontrol—that is, removing unnecessary layers of review and delegating authority to the operating level so that those who did the work had the tools they needed to succeed. Although the HHS effort clearly complied with the White House directive, it really operated on a separate track and did not actually touch the core of the department's policy activities.[51]

Y2K. By late summer 1998, it was becoming clear that the federal government could face major problems if it did not act to ensure that internal computer systems and those of organizations with which they work were year 2000 (Y2K) compliant. A major effort to avoid any computer crises on January 1, 2000, was organized out of the Executive Office of the President, largely through OMB, working with the President's Management Council to provide leadership and support efforts within all the federal departments and agencies.

By November 1999 work was already completed on more than 99 percent of all critical computer systems, including those used in air traffic control, Social Security payments, and the country's critical infrastructure areas. The HHS leadership joined other federal officials in reporting on progress. Contingency plans were devised and any problems with the conversion were avoided.

Efforts were developed within HHS at three levels. The first involved the department's own systems (payments and other priorities critical to its mission). The second highlighted the work of the partners involved in carrying out the work of the department (state agencies and other partners). And the third level involved the program sectors themselves, ensuring that the department's programs could be carried out (for example, ensuring an adequate supply of pharmaceuticals).[52]

The Appointments Process

Over the past several decades the placement of political officials in the federal agencies has been the responsibility of the presidential appointments office within the White House Office of Presidential Personnel. That office is usually most active at the beginning of a presidential term and has to balance the need to staff agencies with appropriate officials with the imperative to place individuals active in the campaign in jobs. In addition, depending on the agency, a new administration will want to give positions to individuals who share its policy perspective. These individuals not only occupy top positions within the agencies but also include those selected to be regional directors of the ten HHS regional offices. The regional directors are frequently individuals who have been involved in the presidential campaign and have valued political contacts with the states in the region.

Because of the volatility of many HHS programs and policies, the White House has often played an active role in identifying and placing individuals in the subcabinet positions. At times this has resulted in difficult situations in which the subcabinet officials are more responsive and loyal to the White House staff than they are to the HHS secretary. At other times, teams have been assembled composed of individuals who are expert in their fields, loyal to the secretary, and able to operate in a highly collegial fashion.[53] The latter situation is possible when the secretary has a close relationship with the presidential team and is able to play a major role in the selection of political staff, perhaps with a veto power over White House selections.

Electoral Politics

Most occupants of the White House find it extremely important to focus on the election calendar; congressional elections, state-level gubernatorial elections, and presidential reelection realities make up the lifeblood for success of an administration. The calendar and pressures that emerge from this reality often collide with a calendar that seems to make sense to a cabinet or program official focusing on program implementation details and ongoing relationships with specialized interest groups.

HHS programs and policies have frequently been affected by the imperatives of electoral politics. Issues have emerged as top priorities not because of some substantive reason but because they relate to political players. Pressures are placed on agencies to develop policies at or by a certain time. Such pressures have sometimes resulted in inadequately analyzed or vetted policies or in the placement of important issues on the back burner.

CONCLUSION

The discussion in this chapter illustrates the range of political actors who can make accountability demands on a cabinet official. Each of these actors may have a different method of expressing such demands. Some ways are related to the structure of government, some to the electoral process, some to the relationships that flow from partisanship, and others to the dynamics of interest group politics.

Although each of them—interest groups, Congress, and the White House—relates to the HHS secretary in its own terms, all of them are crucial to the cabinet official's survival.

Raymond Wilson has learned that he cannot ignore any of the political actors within his universe. Each of these players has the ability to create problems for him; he has to be flexible enough to respond to their concerns. Once again he returns to the juggling metaphor and realizes that he cannot drop any of the political actors around him. Even if he cannot satisfy all of their substantive demands, he knows that they all have to believe they have an opportunity to be heard by him. Because of changes over time, he needs a strategy that will give him as much of an early warning system as is possible. This early warning system can involve not only actors outside the department but the career staff within HHS, which, he realizes, has access to good information about specific program developments. And because of the size and diversity of the department, he needs to assemble a political team that shares a set of values and approaches. He hopes that he will be able to play a major role in this selection process with the support of the White House and relevant congressional actors. One of the major elements in developing political relationships is the presence of trust. It will be a challenge for him to create a supportive environment for the creation of such trust.

Notes

1. James W. Fesler and Donald F. Kettl, *The Politics of the Administrative Process,* 2d ed. (Chatham, N.J.: Chatham House, 1996), 15.

2. Mark H. Moore, *Creating Public Value: Strategic Management in Government* (Cambridge: Harvard University Press, 1995), chap. 5.

3. Alexis de Tocqueville, *Democracy in America,* vol. 1 (New York: Vintage Books, 1954), 202.

4. Louis C. Gawthrop, *Bureaucratic Behavior in the Executive Branch* (New York: Free Press, 1969), 79–80.

5. Hugh Heclo, "Issue Networks and the Executive Establishment," in *The New American Political System,* ed. Anthony King (Washington, D.C.: American Enterprise Institute for Public Policy Research, 1979), 87–124.

6. James Q. Wilson, *Bureaucracy: What Government Agencies Do and Why They Do It* (New York: Basic Books, 1989), 76–78.

7. John W. Kingdon, *Agendas, Alternatives, and Public Policies,* 2d ed. (New York: HarperCollins, 1995), 48–49.

8. Wilson, *Bureaucracy,* 84.

9. William P. Browne, *Groups, Interests, and U.S. Public Policy* (Washington, D.C.: Georgetown University Press, 1998), 231–232.

10. See Web site http://www.aarp.org.

11. See Web site http://www.unos.org.

12. See discussion of various players in the policy process in Kingdon, *Agendas, Alternatives, and Public Policies.*

13. See Peter Edelman, *Searching for America's Heart* (New York: Houghton Mifflin, 2001) for a discussion of the welfare policy controversy.

14. A. Lee Fritschler, *Smoking and Politics: Policymaking and the Federal Bureaucracy,* 3d ed. (Englewood Cliffs, N.J.: Prentice Hall, 1983), 6.

15. Ibid., 23–24.

16. Ibid., 24.

17. See Stanton A. Glantz, John Slade, Lisa A. Bero, Peter Hanauer, and Deborah E. Barnes, *The Cigarette Papers* (Berkeley: University of California Press, 1996), chap. 2.

18. David Kessler, *A Question of Intent: A Great American Battle with a Deadly Industry* (Washington, D.C.: Public Affairs Press, 2001).

19. See Joel D. Aberbach, *Keeping a Watchful Eye: The Politics of Congressional Oversight* (Washington, D.C.: Brookings Institution, 1990).

20. See discussion in Beryl A. Radin and Joan Price Boase, "Federalism, Political Structure, and Public Policy in the United States and Canada," *Journal of Comparative Policy Analysis* 2 (2000): 65–89.

21. Aberbach, *Keeping a Watchful Eye,* 11.

22. Allen Schick, *The Federal Budget: Politics, Policy, Process,* rev. ed. (Washington, D.C.: Brookings Institution, 2000), 175.

23. Wilson, *Bureaucracy,* 238.

24. Ibid., 250.

25. Bernard Rosen, *Holding Government Bureaucracies Accountable,* 3d ed. (Westport, Conn.: Praeger, 1998), 66.

26. U.S. General Accounting Office, *Confirmation of Political Appointees: Eliciting Nominees' Views on Leadership and Management Issues,* report to the Chairman, Subcommittee on Oversight of Government Management, Restructuring, and the District of Columbia, Committee on Governmental Affairs, U.S. Senate, GAO/GGD-00-174, August 2000.

27. John H. Trattner, *The 2000 Prune Book: How to Succeed in Washington's Top Jobs* (Washington, D.C.: Council for Excellence in Government and Brookings Institution Press, 2000).

28. Jane Henney, quoted in ibid., 222.

29. Trattner, *The 2000 Prune Book,* 230, 235.

30. Schick, *The Federal Budget: Politics, Policy, Process,* 1.

31. Ibid., 2.

32. Rosen, *Holding Government Bureaucracies Accountable,* 66.

33. Schick, *The Federal Budget: Politics, Policy, Process,* 18.

34. Trattner, *The 2000 Prune Book,* 230.

35. House Committee on Appropriations, Subcommittee on the Departments of Labor, Health and Human Services, Education, and Related Agencies, *Hearings on the National Institutes of Health,* comments of NIH director Harold Varmus, April 19, 1994, 18, quotation on p. 3.

36. Robert Herbert, "The Quiet Scourge," *New York Times,* January 11, 2001, A25.

37. See Beryl A. Radin, "The Government Performance and Results Act (GPRA) and the Tradition of Federal Management Reform: Square Pegs in Round Holes?" *Journal of Public Administration Research and Theory* 10 (January 2000).

38. Quoted in Rosen, *Holding Government Bureaucracies Accountable*, 69.

39. Aberbach, *Keeping a Watchful Eye*, 138.

40. Ibid., 47.

41. Aberbach, quoted in ibid., 7.

42. Burdett Loomis, quoted in Paul C. Light, *Monitoring Government: Inspectors General and the Search for Accountability* (Washington, D.C.: Brookings Institution, 1993), 40.

43. Trattner, *The 2000 Prune Book*, 231.

44. Joe Stephens and Valerie Strauss, "CDC Concedes 'Mistake' in Misleading Congress," *Washington Post*, February 3, 2000, A21. Also Joe Stephens and Valerie Strauss, "CDC Director Plans Audits and Overhaul," *Washington Post*, February 11, 2000, A39.

45. Rufus E. Miles Jr., *The Department of H.E.W.* (New York: Praeger, 1974), 266.

46. Fesler and Kettl, *The Politics of the Administrative Process*, 101.

47. Other areas within OMB authority also have an impact on the decision-making process inside a department. These include the regulatory review process, management issues, and review of speeches and congressional testimony.

48. Fesler and Kettl, *The Politics of the Administrative Process*, 103.

49. Shelley Lynn Tomkin, *Inside OMB: Politics and Process in the President's Budget Office* (Armonk, N.Y.: M. E. Sharpe, 1998), 79.

50. See Theda Skocpol, *Boomerang: Clinton's Health Security Effort and the Turn Against Government in U.S. Politics* (New York: Norton, 1996) for a description of the process.

51. See Beryl A. Radin, "Varieties of Reinvention: Six NPR 'Success Stories,'" in *Inside the Reinvention Machine*, ed. John DiIulio and Donald Kettl (Washington, D.C.: Brookings Institution, 1995).

52. Beryl A. Radin, *The Challenge of Managing Across Boundaries: The Case of the Office of the Secretary in the U.S. Department of Health and Human Services*, Grant Report, PricewaterhouseCoopers Endowment for the Business of Government, November 2000, 16–18.

53. Beryl A. Radin, *Managing Decentralized Departments: The Case of the U.S. Department of Health and Human Services*, Grant Report, PricewaterhouseCoopers Endowment for the Business of Government, October 1999, 13.

6

Accountability and
Management Processes

THE ADVICE that Raymond Wilson has received from his
predecessors leaves him puzzled. Several of them emphasized the
importance of getting control over the department. They expressed frustration about the independence of units within the
agency, some of which had longer and stronger relationships
with interest groups and congressional members and staff than
did the secretary. Those former secretaries had built up the staff
and capacities of the centralized units within the Office of the
Secretary. They viewed those units as their arsenal to control the
units through management processes. By contrast, other of his
predecessors had employed exactly the opposite strategy. They
advised him to be realistic about the limited ability of any secretary to control the multiple units within the department and, instead, to employ a strategy that assumed decentralization.

Wilson also notes that his predecessors had approached the
management task with very different assumptions about potential differences between the public and private sectors. Several of
the previous secretaries had moved into the role with essentially
no experience in public sector organizations. They viewed the
job as a management challenge and thought they could bring
their past experience in the private sector to the task. For others,
their public sector experience had been in the political sphere as
elected officials at the federal level (members of Congress) or as
governors.

Wilson isn't sure exactly how he fits into this picture. He had
been the chief executive officer (CEO) of a very large, urban
public hospital in California. Managing such an enterprise made
him realize that he was dependent on the medical staff to carry

out many of the initiatives that he thought would be effective. Although hospital managers play important roles in regard to financial and personnel processes, they have to be sensitive to the limits of their ability to influence the behavior of physicians, particularly those in high-status specializations.

And when he went to the Department of Health as state health director, he also realized that the state agency had limited authority to control programs that were administered (and sometimes partially financed) by counties. Yet the first press accounts about his California appointment characterized him as a skilled manager who would be able to take control of a state agency that had been the subject of much criticism. Despite his limited authority, if a crisis or emergency occurred anywhere in the system, the state agency in Sacramento was held publicly responsible for dealing with it.

Wilson thinks that his California experience will serve him well as a manager. He recognizes that large public organizations provide limited opportunities for traditional approaches to management that are drawn from the private sector. He is aware that the top official in a highly visible and volatile public agency lives in a fish bowl and can expect a high level of public scrutiny about what might be viewed as traditional management prerogatives.

As he approaches the confirmation hearings, he knows that the management issues that are important to him are not likely to be raised during those sessions, yet he can't forget about them. He reminds himself of those questions:

- Is it possible to devise a clear strategy for the department that emphasizes the role of the Office of the Secretary? How should the secretary think about the department's multiple cultures and balance centralized approaches with decentralized efforts?
- How can the secretary develop an approach that is flexible enough to respond to unexpected or crisis issues that are likely to emerge?
- Are there ways that the secretary can identify high-risk programs within the department (that is, programs that are more difficult to implement than others)?
- How should the secretary approach the multiple processes and units that are found within the department to provide information about the legal and fiscal performance of program units?

THIS CHAPTER includes discussion of many management issues that are related to the HHS accountability task. It includes public/private differences, the context of the management task, and the special characteristics of HHS that are important. It also focuses on the role of the units in the Office of the Secretary within a decentralized setting as well as sources of oversight for the secretary.

PUBLIC/PRIVATE DIFFERENCES

Much of the day-to-day activity that defines what a cabinet secretary does has strong parallels to the job of a CEO in the private sector. But as both Wallace Sayre and Graham Allison have noted, public and private management are fundamentally alike in all unimportant respects.[1] Selma Mushkin's list of public management elements contains functions and tasks that clearly suggest affinities to the private sector. These include personnel management, collective bargaining and labor management relations, productivity and performance measurement, organization and reorganization, financial management, evaluation research, and program and management audit.[2] The generic management functions outlined by Gulick and Urwick in their classic *Papers in the Science of Administration* (known as POSDCORB) are not unfamiliar to managers in both sectors. These include planning, organizing, staffing, directing, coordinating, reporting, and budgeting.[3]

The analogy to the CEO's responsibilities is appealing, intriguing, and often misleading. Mark H. Moore has suggested that "[t]he image of success in public management as achieving one's own policy objectives leaves managers too little scope to learn what others want and too much freedom to dominate the process with idiosyncratic views of the public interest."[4] Former cabinet official Robert B. Reich describes the public management task within a democratic system as different from private-sector management and different from public management in an undemocratic society. He suggests that public sector managers have to balance effectiveness, responsiveness, and deliberation as they devise their activities.[5]

Former treasury secretary W. Michael Blumenthal reflected on his transition from the private sector to the public arena in an article in *Fortune* magazine. He noted that "the head of a government department or agency is not like the chief executive of a large corporation who has control over the personnel system, who can change it, can instill a certain spirit, can hire and fire. In government, that kind of control does not exist." Yet, he went on, "it's still true that some of the basic rules that I learned and applied successfully in business and hope to apply again when I return to business, are equally important in government, except they are not the only things that are required for success. Business is simple to succeed in if you follow a few simple rules. Government is harder."[6]

Moore has highlighted the role of the public sector manager as a political manager. He focuses on the role of these managers as entrepreneurs who "increase the public value produced by public sector organizations in both the short and the long run." He uses the metaphor of *explorers* to describe what he thinks about the proper role of public sector executives. The role, he comments, is

> tied much more closely to the reality of modern governance but geared to preserving, even enhancing, the ideas of democratic accountability. In this image, public executives are neither clerks nor martyrs. Instead, they are *explorers* commissioned by society to search for public value. In undertaking the search, managers are expected to use their initiative and imagination. But they are also expected to be responsive to more or less constant political guidance and feedback. Their most important ethical responsibility is to undertake the search for public value conscientiously.[7]

Interviews with nine managers of large government agencies emphasized what they called four key characteristics of public sector leaders. These included a sense of urgency, a "mental model" of effective organizations based on prior work experience, a division of the future organization, and a drive to put that vision in place.[8] These interviews were used to develop a checklist of the qualities to seek in political appointees charged with running agencies. In addition, they were also suggested as attributes to think about to help career officials understand the reality of the political leader.

THE CONTEXT OF THE MANAGEMENT RESPONSIBILITIES

Public organizations that are in operation at the beginning of the twenty-first century exhibit characteristics that are quite different from those organizations that were found during most of the twentieth century. A snapshot of such organizations—particularly those operating at the federal government level—provides a picture that is without a clear visual focus. It is often difficult to ascertain which aspects of the organization are in the foreground of the picture and which aspects are in the background.

This creates a real challenge for a new secretary of a cabinet department. Not only are these organizations extremely complex but they are increasingly charged with the implementation of a variety of policies and programs, employing a range of instruments to accomplish their objective. Increasingly federal organizations do not actually carry out the service delivery function themselves but, rather, rely on others (actors in other levels of the public sector as well as those in the private and nonprofit sectors) to carry out the mission of the organization. The combination of complexity and involvement of others creates a sense of increased uncertainty for top managers, who must respond to constantly changing circumstances.

Although some degree of complexity has always characterized federal organizations (and formal structures have never really described what happens inside an organization), the extent of this complexity has increased over the past decade. Most recently, the determination to flatten organizations, reduce hierarchies, and devolve responsibilities for implementation of programs to others, has contributed to this situation. As a result, the techniques and approaches that have been used in the past to manage large public organizations require rethinking.

In the past, management of these organizations relied on two major approaches: tinkering with organizational structure and adopting centralized processes as control mechanisms.

Changes in Organizational Structure. Modifications to the organizational structure have traditionally been used as a way of linking programs or units together or to limit the autonomy of specific units. The reorganizations that emerge from this strategy provide a mechanism for those charged with the management responsibility within a large umbrella agency to minimize fragmentation and establish consistencies across program units. The assumption has been that centralization will solve most problems.

Although some reorganization efforts have been openly devised as methods of controlling what are viewed as maverick or runaway agencies, most of these efforts have been promoted as attempts to increase efficiency or provide approaches that would achieve policy or program effectiveness.[9] At the same time, agencies are often wary of embarking on a major reorganization because it usually causes a period of disruption within the agency. In addition, agencies are constrained by Congress in their ability to make major changes in structure solely on management grounds.

Centralized Management Processes. Traditionally a series of internal management processes has been used to highlight consistencies and efficiencies within large agencies composed of multiple and diffuse units. The budget process is most commonly used to play this role, providing a way for top offices of a department or large agency to establish command and control mechanisms that minimize the autonomy of units in their search for fiscal resources. Units have usually come to centralized budget offices as supplicants for those resources. Similarly, both the personnel process and the acquisition process have been employed to achieve this purpose, providing mechanisms in which a centralized unit in the large organization plays a controlling role, limiting the discretion of the smaller units. Over the years, the growth of staff units within the top reaches of federal agencies has been a response to this urge.

By the end of the twentieth century, however, the limitations of these strategies have been acknowledged by many who have responsibility for federal management reform. Through the various efforts that have been associated with the reinvention movement (the National Performance Review and other reform efforts) the pendulum has swung away from reform that increased centralization and emphasized a command and control approach to management. As Osborne and Gaebler have described it, organizations have adopted the "steer not row" approach to management.[10]

Thus, in this context, to continue to rely on the traditional modes of achieving a corporate identity in large-scale federal agencies seems to be foolhardy. Although these strategies have not been completely rejected, new approaches have been developed as alternative ways of managing these structures. The tools available to deal with these issues usually lie within the Office of the Secretary of a department—that is, in the staff rather than line components of the department. Some of the techniques that have been employed are not new, but because they are used in a context of decentralization, they take on a meaning different from that in the past.

Rather than emphasizing structural centralization or command and control strategies, proponents of these approaches have sought to find a way to define a role for top management in the context of decentralized, flat, and devolved organizations. Although the majority of the energy and work of these organizations is done in the decentralized units, there are times when it is important to find a way for the top management to become involved in activities, playing a coordination or crosscutting role.

MANAGING HHS

The management job in HHS is a formidable one. And it is often difficult to separate the criticisms and problems dealing with management in this department from the role that it plays in the American society and the controversies surrounding its programs. As he departed from the job of HEW secretary, Joseph Califano reflected on his experience:

> It has become as fashionable to attack Washington today as it was to attack Brooklyn when I was a kid. Government is not the enemy of the people; government is the servant of the people. The important thing is to recognize that in a free society there are certain limited numbers of things that government does. By and large, most of those things can be done by no one else, and the things that this Department does and is charged to do are things for people who cannot find help anywhere else.[11]

As former HHS secretary Donna Shalala wrote, "Managing a large organization is the art of the possible, the art of finding the possible within what might be viewed as impossible pressures. Between . . . two extremes—that nothing works or that everything can be made to work—lies some basic truths about large modern organizations."[12]

Shalala, the secretary during the Clinton administration, adopted a conscious management strategy that was very different from those attempted in the past.

She began with the assumption that the department contains many decentralized elements and that it is not possible to change them. She described the department as composed of many units that have their own history, needs, cultures, and constituencies. She used the professional credibility of the subunits within the office (especially those dealing with the health world) as an important source of public and political support. She downsized the Office of the Secretary and delegated many different functions to the operating components (this general approach was clearly rationalized by the reform strategy of Vice President Gore's National Performance Review).[13] At the same time, she attempted to devise processes that emphasized coordination and identify areas in which crosscutting approaches are essential. Her efforts represented an attempt to change the ways in which the department is managed and, as a result, to improve internal and external effectiveness of its operations.

Despite efforts that spanned several decades, the strategies that had been employed by past secretaries over the years were not able to deal with the predictable realities of the department's external environment or with predictable internal dynamics. These are forces that any secretary must confront. The external environment challenges management in many different ways: the diversity and size of operating programs; the reality of vague and difficult goals; fragmented accountability structures and program authority; different program responsibilities; controversial issues; and diverse constituencies. The forces that emerge from internal dynamics include multiple policy perspectives; conflicting policy approaches; staff-line competition; and "gaming" filtering units. The flexible strategy that was employed by Secretary Shalala appeared to be more effective in dealing with these forces than efforts that had been tried in the past.

Four of the many management concerns that require the attention of the HHS secretary are particularly noteworthy. These are issues that deal with organization structure, personnel issues, the role of the Office of the Secretary, and mechanisms for internal oversight.

Organization Structure

Since its creation in 1953 as an amalgam of several existing agencies, HHS (and its predecessor, HEW) struggled with the appropriate balance between centralized functions in the Office of the Secretary and autonomy in the various agencies and bureaus contained within its boundaries. Over the years, the pendulum has swung back and forth between centralization and decentralization as an either implicit or explicit management strategy.[14]

It has been observed that reorganization of administrative structures—changing the balance between centralized and decentralized approaches—has become a regular feature of contemporary bureaucratic life. March and Olsen have commented that "the history of administrative reorganization in the twentieth century is a history of rhetoric."[15] Most major reorganizations in the federal government have involved the White House and Congress. However, organizational shifts occur regularly within departments and agencies, reflecting changes in the responsibilities of government as well as the effort by cabinet officials to redirect the way in which management functions are carried out.

The formal structure of contemporary organizations often masks ambiguity and conflict. Although specialized units have been brought together under a common umbrella or framework, one needs simply to scratch the surface of those organizations to recognize that it is often illusory to think of those umbrellas as an accurate way of describing what actually goes on within the organizational structure.

Mechanisms are required that allow a cabinet official to be able to act relatively quickly as new problems arise, to avoid establishing management processes for their own sakes, to focus strategically with a specific set of policy or program goals, and to deal with a variety of actors both inside and outside the department. In addition, the cabinet secretary often needs to develop procedures that are time limited and crafted to deal with a specific issue.

As has been discussed, over the years, the structure of HHS has changed significantly, reflecting changes in priorities and the addition of new programs to the department's portfolio. The organization chart that was in place in the 1970s bears little resemblance to the structure at the turn of the twenty-first century.[16]

For example, two large units are no longer found within the department's umbrella; the creation of a separate Department of Education in 1979 and a spinning off of the Social Security Administration to independent status in 1995 removed large units from the department's responsibilities.

But in addition to the removal of these two units, many program areas have been reordered, renamed, and reconceptualized. In the 1970s an assistant secretary for human development (AHD) had responsibility for programs dealing with youth, children, and aging. In the 1990s the programs for children and families were located within the Office of the Assistant Secretary for the Administration for Children and Families, and the programs dealing with welfare were moved from what had been the Social and Rehabilitation Service to ACF. The Administration on Aging was moved out of AHD into a separate entity and a Health Care Financing Administration had responsibility for Medicare, Medicaid, and the Child Health Insurance Program.

In the 1970s six organizational units were found under the umbrella of the Public Health Service, headed by an assistant secretary for health (who at times was also the surgeon general). These included the NIH, the FDA, the CDC, and three agencies that have been since renamed: the Health Resources Administration; the Health Services Administration; and the Alcohol, Drug Abuse, and Mental Health Administration. The latter three have been restructured as the

Health Resources and Services Administration and the Substance Abuse and Mental Health Services Administration.

The organization chart at the end of the 1990s did not have an assistant secretary for health as a line manager. Rather, the FDA, the NIH, HRSA, the CDC, SAMHSA, a newly elevated Indian Health Service, and a newly created unit called the Agency for Healthcare Research and Quality all reported directly to the secretary. Although some critics are concerned that too many entities fall under the secretary's control, in reality many actually did so in the past; many of the program units that had reported to the assistant secretary for health actually had their own separate relationship with the secretary and a high level of discretion and autonomy, even though the organization chart suggested that they did not have an independent path to the secretary. There still is an assistant secretary for health, but that person serves as a staff—rather than a line—adviser to the secretary. When the Social Security Administration was moved out of HHS, it left a large segment of the department's programs under a line assistant secretary for health, competing with the secretary for influence over those programs.

Most of the changes involving organizational structure in HHS have focused on function (purpose, clientele, or process) rather than on area (place).[17] Although the department has ten regional offices spread across the country, over the years the level of formal authority and responsibility for program operations varied tremendously by program component. During the early 1970s the department made an effort to give regional directors more responsibility over program operations, viewing them as mini-secretaries who would be participants in the departmental policy-making process.[18] Despite this effort, there was always tension between the regional program officials, who usually reported to their program counterparts in Washington, and the generalist regional director, who sought to speak for the department as a whole. At one point, a proposal was floated to eliminate the regional offices altogether.

Over the years, the size of the regional staffs has diminished significantly, and decisions that might have been made at the regional level have been moved to Washington (or, in the case of the CMS, to Baltimore). As some grant programs were folded into block grants rather than categorical grants, there was less authority within the program structure to deal with the details of program operations. At least one of the program units (SAMHSA) does not currently have regional staff. Although CDC staff are stationed across the country (often assigned to state and local health departments), they do not operate out of the regional offices.

Personnel Issues

As former treasury secretary Michael Blumenthal noted, one of the clearest differences between the private and public sectors relates to the extent of the ability of the chief executive to direct personnel and the personnel management system.[19] A private sector executive has the ability to hire and fire and to establish the criteria for the individuals who will become a part of the organization. A public sector manager has to operate within the civil service system, a system that— according to Fesler and Kettl—has many managers.[20] Within the federal government, responsibilities for the civil service are distributed among a number of executive-branch agencies. Since 1978 the central agency with this responsibility has been the Office of Personnel Management (OPM). Over the years, however, particularly during the Clinton administration, in a move away from a single standard for recruiting, hiring, and promoting staff across the federal government, much of the personnel or human resources authority was delegated to departments and agencies. These changes were an effort to change what some viewed as "excessive standardization, centralization, and procedural complexities."[21]

This delegation of personnel authority did not, however, result in a highly flexible system that is responsive to a cabinet secretary. A cabinet secretary continues to be constrained by personnel policies and directives that are contained within appropriations bills and through other congressional action. And in other instances, personnel determinations are further limited by directives of the Executive Office of the President, especially through OMB policies that seek to establish government-wide approaches (such as freezes on hiring or requirements for reduction in staffing levels).

The attributes that constrain the autonomy of a cabinet secretary are often the very elements that make up the elements of a civil service system. A civil service system seeks to devise a personnel system that is focused on merit, training, and experience and that provides opportunities for individuals regardless of attributes such as race, gender, age, or ethnicity. Focusing on rules that flow from classification of specific requirements for jobs, such a system attempts to avoid individual differences that are not viewed as relevant to the performance of a specific job. Although these rules and procedures reflect commendable values, they can act to minimize the discretion of the secretary.

Unlike the systems found in many other countries, the American system also constrains the career civil service by creating a layer of political appointees above the career staffers. Some of these individuals require Senate confirmation; more, however, do not require Senate confirmation and are appointed to their positions because of contacts in the White House or with the cabinet secretary. These individuals are often viewed as the facilitators for an administration's policy or political agenda. Despite criticisms of the scope and size of this political layer, it has continued to be one of the characteristics of the American political system and has contributed to what is often described as unproductive conflict between career and political officials.[22]

HHS secretaries have dealt with personnel issues in quite different ways. Some secretaries have attempted to exert strong control over these questions by appointing individuals who do not trust or, at the least, are skeptical about the values of the career bureaucracy. This approach is most likely to be found at the early stages of a new administration, when new officials of a political party different from its predecessor believe that the career bureaucracy is tainted with the policies of the previous administration. This is particularly problematic when political officials are appointed less for their expertise in a field and more for their political loyalty. Given the permeability of the system (especially involving Congress and interest groups), in the long run this can prove to be quite counterproductive to a secretary's agenda if those who speak for the secretary are not comfortable dealing with the details of policy.

Other HHS secretaries have valued the career bureaucracy and have sought to avoid conflict between the political and career staff. In recent years, delays in naming and confirming second tier subcabinet staff have created opportunities for civil servants as well as the necessity of relying on them. Former HHS secretary Donna Shalala has written that she started her career in the department with many of the top jobs unfilled. As a result, she noted that the department was run by the top civil servants—"the people who are responsible for most of our day-to-day leadership." Further, she noted, the relationship between career and political officials is reciprocal. "Both institutional and political guidance are needed. Trust can be built by using the experience and institutional memories of career civil servants . . . . We need to make sure we respect the integrity of the civil service in words and action."[23]

Another aspect of personnel issues that is extremely relevant for an HHS secretary involves the degree to which authority for personnel decisions is delegated to the program components within the department. The diversity of staff required for specific program units is sometimes overwhelming. This is particularly true in those agencies that hire a large number of scientists. In an agency such as the NIH's National Cancer Institute it is essential for personnel policy to be established by individuals who understand the reality of the science and research task. During the late 1990s, policies were put in place that ended what was viewed as a culture conflict between the administrative staff of the agency and the science staff. This resulted in the attraction of new scientists to the institute, using systems that provided opportunities to bring in both senior and junior scientists to the organization.

THE OFFICE OF THE SECRETARY

As has been noted earlier, when the federal government's involvement in social programs increased dramatically in the 1960s, new attention was focused on the operations of the Department of Health, Education and Welfare. By the mid-

1960s, however, the Office of the Secretary had emerged as a force within the department. The span of activity grew wider as the federal government became a more important force in the society. Building on two processes—controlling the budget and determining departmental positions on legislation—the Office of the Secretary grew and tried to bring together the separate forces within the program components and reach for a common set of policy goals within the department. For the most part, the assistant secretaries in the department were used primarily as staff officers whose role was to help the secretary knit together related functions in the operating agencies.

Management efforts within the department thus reflected an approach that emphasized control, monitoring, consistency in operations and approaches, and clarity about lines of authority. From that time on, most secretaries of HHS have searched for management systems that provide policy leadership and, as well, offer a way for them to oversee departmental administrative matters and programs. In a few cases, efforts at management reform have accentuated attempts to identify interdependencies and shared issues across program elements. Most efforts, however, emphasized modes of control of the separate elements within the department.

This agenda drew on several strategies. In some cases, the attempt to control the program components was done through manipulation of the organization structure, moving program components into new configurations in which they were required to work with previously separate and autonomous elements. For example, most of the department's health programs were moved into a newly configured Office of the Assistant Secretary for Health in 1968. More frequently, however, the control agenda was achieved through formalized processes of budget development, planning, policy analysis, personnel, procurement, legislative development, public affairs, and legal advice by the general counsel. Through the years, various management techniques (such as the Planning, Programming, and Budgeting System, known as PPBS) became the instrumentality for the processes. In some cases the control agenda was achieved by focusing on the substance of specific policy initiatives. Former secretary Califano put a variation of a management-by-objectives approach in place, creating what he called the Major Initiatives Tracking System (MITS)—a technique that established numerical goals by which to judge the performance of individuals and to inspire them to greater productivity and efficiency.[24]

A report issued by the General Accounting Office in 1990 depicts the approach that was predominant until 1993. This report on management in HHS was published in the GAO series of management reviews of major departments and agencies. The intent of the report was to assess the role and effectiveness of the Office of the Secretary in managing the department and to identify ways in which departmental management processes and structures could be improved. The GAO focused on the lack of what it called "an effective management system within the Office of the Secretary." [25] According to the GAO, a management system should be able to identify issues, define goals and objectives, develop strategies, create monitoring systems, oversee operations, and receive feedback on performance. In its analysis, the GAO wrote that the efforts within the department did not go far enough and that HHS was not able to create a system that actually required the operating programs to respond to the will of the secretary. The GAO found that the lack of departmental strategic planning was a "key element missing" from the HHS system.

Although the GAO report did acknowledge some of the forces and constraints that made it difficult to encourage central management in HHS, it was clear that the GAO analysts sought ways to overcome these difficulties. GAO also argued that it was possible to differentiate between two types of planning—strategic and operational—and to cast the role of the Office of the Secretary in the strategic planning mode, which would set the framework for the operational planning role performed by the program units.

The report pointed to some systems that had moved in the preferred direction but noted that "[n]o secretarial management system has stayed intact long enough to provide stability to the Department's basic operations." [26] At the time the report was written, a senior level advisory body called the Management Council provided a biweekly venue for the senior staff of the department to meet with the secretary. In the past, department-wide planning processes such as PPBS and the Cooperative Agency Management System (CAMS) had attempted to provide a department-wide perspective. Creation of the Executive Secretariat—an office that circulated policy proposals to appropriate parties within the department—provided a mechanism for clearance of policy positions and documents (especially regulations).

Traditionally a series of internal management processes has been used to highlight consistencies and efficiencies within large agencies composed of multiple and diffuse units. The budget process is most commonly used to play this role, providing a way for top offices of a department or large agency to establish command and control mechanisms that minimize the autonomy of units in their search for fiscal resources. Units have usually come to centralized budget offices as supplicants for those resources. Similarly, both the personnel process and the acquisition process have been employed to achieve this purpose, providing mechanisms in which a centralized unit in the large organization plays a controlling role, limiting the discretion of the smaller units. Over the years, the growth of staff units within the top reaches of federal agencies has been a response to this urge for control.

Increasingly, those who have employed structural reorganization strategies recognize that these efforts may be less substantive than symbolic. Moving a unit around within a larger organizational framework may have little impact on the way the unit actually does its work. Similarly, the attempt to manage large-scale federal organizations through centralized units has neither been very effective nor has it comported with the fragmented decision-making process that characterizes the American political system. Although the press and some legislative critics focus on the role of the secretary or the top organizational leader in an agency, decisions related to resources (particularly the budget) and legislative authority are made in the context of the specialized units within the umbrella organization. At times, however, some centralization of specific functions is the only effective way to address problems.

Thus, in this context, to continue to rely on the traditional modes of achieving a corporate identity in large-scale federal agencies seems to be foolhardy. Although these strategies have not been completely rejected, new approaches have been developed as alternative ways of managing these structures. The tools available to deal with these issues usually lie within the Office of the Secretary of a department—that is, in the staff rather than the line components of the department. Some of the techniques that have been employed are not new, but because they are used in a context of decentralization, they take on a different meaning from the one they had in the past.

Rather than emphasizing structural centralization or command and control strategies, these approaches sought to find a way to define a role for top management in the context of decentralized, flat, and devolved organizations. Although the majority of the work of these organizations was done in the decentralized units, there were times when it was important to find a way for the top management to become involved in activities, playing a coordinating or crosscutting role.

Several examples from the Clinton administration illustrate a modified way of managing a large federal department. Some of these examples illustrate efforts at institutionalizing processes that both respect the autonomy of the decentralized units and provide a role for the Office of the Secretary and top management of the department. Still other examples reflect specific policy or program issues that require the department to play a role, either because of external pressure or because of conflicts between approaches taken by units within the department.

Four types of crosscutting mechanisms were used: mechanisms for problem solving; mechanisms for coordination; mechanisms for information sharing and team building; and processes to balance a bottom-up and department-wide perspective.[27] These examples indicate that it is possible to devise ways for the Office of the Secretary to become involved in the department's decision process without resorting to command and control approaches. The roles that emerge from this strategy include seeking long-term solutions, broadening an issue, serving as a facilitator, encouraging bottom-up efforts, and translating technical issues to generalist language.

This strategy acknowledges that care must be taken in the way that program units are treated; they must be respected, not tolerated. Crosscutting and coordinating mechanisms within the Office of the Secretary must be devised with modest expectations. Not all areas are appropriate for an active Office of the Secretary role, and it is important to work hard to avoid preempting the program units. At the same time, these approaches do provide a way for the Office of the Secretary to add value. They create a set of roles in a diverse agency that allows it to develop a corporate identity in which the whole is greater than the sum of the parts.

Responding to White House Calls for Crosscutting: The HHS Data Council

In March 1995 Vice President Gore asked HHS to develop a departmental response to issues related to promotion of health care applications in the national information infrastructure. The vice president highlighted four different areas of concern: data standards, privacy, enhanced health information for consumers, and telemedicine. Although the department already had work under way in each of these areas, the request allowed it to consolidate ongoing efforts into a coherent strategy coordinated with other agencies, with attention to private sector and state roles.

The White House request spawned a department-wide information policy initiative, handed to a department-wide committee to develop. That group not only focused on the four areas specified by the vice president but also broadened the scope to focus on the department's own information system policy, moving away from categorical program-specific activities to a more integrated and cohesive approach to these issues.

By December 1995 the secretary had created a formal body called the Data Council to reflect the reorganized HHS structure. That group would address the full range of health and nonhealth data and privacy questions identified by the working group.

The Data Council's charge was to coordinate all HHS health and nonhealth data collection and analysis activities. Membership on the council was to consist of all assistant secretary and agency administrator-level HHS officials who report directly to the secretary, the HHS privacy advocate, and the secretary's senior adviser on health statistics. It was co-chaired by the assistant secretary for planning and evaluation (located in the Office of the Secretary) and a rotating program head. Each member was asked to appoint an alternate to attend when he or she was not available and a staff contact person to handle communications about Data Council business. Staff for the council was to be provided by the Office of the Assistant Secretary for Planning and Evaluation.

The council developed a six-item agenda that would guide its work:

• Develop a department-wide data collection strategy, including coordination and integration of surveys and oversight of surveys and general statistical analysis.

- Coordinate HHS and inter-department health data standards activities, including the implementation of the Health Insurance Portability and Accountability Act Administrative Simplification effort.
- Serve as HHS liaison for the National Committee on Vital and Health Statistics.
- Serve as a focus for HHS issues relating to privacy of health and social services information.
- Provide a forum for coordination of health and human services issues raised by the expanding national information infrastructure activities.
- Provide a forum for coordination of HHS responses to external requests for HHS action on issues related to health and social services data.

As the Data Council evolved, its mandate became more complex. The passage of the Health Insurance Portability and Accountability Act of 1996 called for the department to develop standards that not only met the new expectations about electronic transmission but also made privacy protections. This latter responsibility required the Data Council to work closely with the National Committee on Vital and Health Statistics, the department's public advisory committee on health data, standards, privacy, and health information policy. In addition, the Data Council was also asked to respond to the need for data to be presented in a form that would provide information on race and ethnicity.

To accomplish these tasks, the Data Council organized itself into working groups. These included the Survey Integration Work Group, the Joint Working Group on Telemedicine, the HHS Privacy Committee, the HHS Committee on Health Data Standards, the Working Group on Racial and Ethnic Data, and the Working Group on International Health Data Collaboration.

To a large extent, the meetings of the Data Council and the working groups were dominated by individuals who focused on the technical aspects of data collection, largely in health. The meetings did provide a forum for individuals with data responsibilities across the department to share concerns and for the exchange of ideas. The agenda that was before the group reinforced this technical tendency.

Although the forum did meet these needs, it also had a down side. Because the health focus of the group so dominated the agenda, there was minimal participation in the deliberations from the human services element in the department. For example, rarely did data issues confronting the Administration on Children and Families come before the data venue.

The Data Council members also found it difficult to translate their concerns to the budget process. Some participants in the process observed that a data strategy approach had not emerged from the council's deliberations. A "wish list," rather than a set of priorities and issues that could be viewed in operational terms, was developed. As a result, data staff in the program units found that the budgets that emerged did not provide them with resources for data collection or with policies that allowed them to move to higher levels of electronic technology. The technical staff, who dominated the Data Council, were not able to translate their concerns in a way that prompted interest by the budget planners at either the individual program unit level or at the departmental level.

By 2000, steps were taken to address these problems. Individuals from the human services side of the department became more involved in Data Council meetings, which were used to help technical data staff understand the intricacies of the budget process. Some of this occurred as a result of increased involvement of individuals from the Office of the Secretary. Although the operational aspects of data issues would continue to be the responsibility of the program units, the presence of staff from the Office of the Secretary helped to broaden the issues and move the activities of the Data Council from a highly specialized focus toward a more generalist orientation.

Avoiding a Crisis and Establishing Norms: Y2K Preparation

Few management issues have commanded the attention that was given to the federal government's efforts to avoid any computer crisis when January 1, 2000, came about. Although there had been some efforts within HHS to plan for the technical conversions that were necessary to prepare for the transition, attention to the issue was located at a fairly low level in the department. It was not until the White House focused on this challenge that the HHS deputy secretary became involved. At the same time, members of Congress held a series of hearings on Y2K issues, focusing public attention on problems that might emerge if the federal agencies were not ready for the conversion.

The President's Management Council began a government-wide effort that was orchestrated by the White House and OMB; a President's Council on Year 2000 Conversion was established, and subgroups were formed to focus on the issues and problems that would be confronted by federal agencies. The HHS deputy secretary chaired the group that focused on transition issues in the health care system.

The initial effort to prepare for the year 2000 was originally viewed as a computer problem. As time went by, it was soon realized that the problem was much broader because of so many system interdependencies and computer functions in devices other than computers (such as medical devices and card key entry systems). By the beginning of 1999, being ready for Y2K was the highest priority in the department.

The deputy secretary's involvement focused on the dimensions of the issue as a problem that cut across the department. He was particularly concerned about keeping continuity of health care intact when the due date came. This would not only involve the department's own computers but also the systems that were found in hospitals and other aspects of the health care system.

Efforts were developed at three levels. The first involved the department's own systems (payments and other mission-critical priorities). The second highlighted the work of the partners involved in carrying out the work of the department (state agencies and other partners). And the third level involved the program sectors themselves, to ensure that the missions of the department's programs could be accomplished (for example, to ensure an adequate supply of pharmaceuticals).

In 1998, working closely with the Office of the Assistant Secretary for Management, the deputy secretary convened biweekly meetings with representatives of the program units. In most instances the chief information officer of a program unit attended the meetings and, in many cases, the program head attended. During these meetings, each element in the department was required to report on what it was doing to prepare for January 1. Following each meeting, a graph was prepared that presented the percentage of compliant Y2K mission-critical systems by program unit. The team's task was to collect and provide information on mission-critical systems, facilities, telecommunications, business continuity and contingency plans, and outreach efforts.

In addition, meetings were held with outside groups that were partners in carrying out HHS program responsibilities. Devolution of responsibilities to state and local governments as well as private and nonprofit groups meant that HHS would not be able to carry out its program mandates unless these groups were ready for the conversion. These included businesses, public service agencies, trade associations, and consumer groups.

The specific tasks required for each program unit varied, depending on the technical systems in place, the structure of the program (if it depended on others to carry out operations), and the level of resources required to make the change. The most complex tasks involved conversion of millions of computer codes within the Health Care Financing Administration, work with field offices and tribal contacts by the Indian Health Service, and conversion of the systems in place at the Food and Drug Administration and the Administration for Children and Families. In addition, the Program Support Center (the unit charged with implementation of payroll and other financial systems) was in the middle of changing to a new computer systems. Given these challenges, efforts were made to focus on agencies with problems.

Although the precise requirements were diverse, the participants in the process recognized that the department would sink or swim as a single unit. During the initial meetings of the department's Y2K team, individuals appeared reluctant to share information, fearing the legal and proprietary problems that might emerge. Some of the program units found the biweekly meetings difficult and were frustrated by the complexity of the task and the time requirement to address the problems. Yet these program staff members knew that the issue was important to the secretary and the deputy secretary and that involvement of top management was essential. As the sessions continued, the participants began to see that they could learn lessons from each other by discussing their experiences.

Before it left the department to become an independent agency, the Social Security Administration (SSA) had begun its compliance activity. Although it was in advance of some of the other department units, it was making these changes on its own and there was no opportunity for others to learn from the SSA. No other part of the department had picked up on the SSA experience.

Involvement of top management also helped the program units to make successful requests for the additional resources required to deal with the conversion. The President's Council on Year 2000 Conversion was able to put pressure on OMB to ensure access to funds outside the regular budget process, and some of the program units received emergency support for conversion activities. The assistant secretary for management and budget (ASMB) acted as the conduit for these funds. By October 1999, the mission-critical systems of all program units were 100 percent compliant in their Y2K conversions.

As January 1 neared, each of the program units and the Office of the Secretary established Day One Centers to monitor the status of the department's systems as well as that of the health care sector and those in the states supporting HHS programs. These centers provided an around-the-clock secure operation capable of receiving reports from the program units, public health organizations, other federal agencies, the pharmaceutical industry, and health care organizations. If required, the centers were able to analyze the reports quickly and provide accurate and timely information to the White House regarding the status of health care and human service sectors. The department also participated in the publication of a booklet for consumers that addressed specific patient and consumer concerns about the delivery of health care after January 1, offered suggestions for what individuals could do to prepare for the transition, and provided consumers with a list of resources for additional information. In addition, technical assistance was provided to state partners, especially by ASMB staff.

Although the department-wide activities were focused on Y2K compliance, the actions that were taken to prepare for the transition created a better understanding of how the department's diverse computer systems work and about the people who operate them. The Y2K effort required each organization in the department to inventory and audit its existing installed base of hardware and software. Systems were identified as mission critical, high impact, obsolete, or in need of upgrades and redesign. In addition, the lessons learned through the Y2K efforts contributed to an understanding of policy, procedure, and security issues that will be addressed by the components of the department in coming years.

Replacing Centralized Budgeting with a Collegial Process: The Budget Review Board

For many years predating the Clinton administration, the budget process within the Office of the Secretary had been the vehicle for exerting a strong, centralized Office of the Secretary perspective. Both program and staff units within the department presented their budget requests in the early summer of each year to a board composed of top officials from the Office of the Secretary. Members of the Budget Review Board (BRB) have traditionally included the ASMB (serving as the chair), the assistant secretary for planning and evaluation (ASPE), the assistant secretary for legislation (ASL), and the assistant secretary for health (ASH).

Prior to the 1995 reorganization the ASH developed a budget that included all the public health components (including the NIH, FDA, and CDC). After that reorganization each of those components presented its own budget individually to the BRB, joining the nonhealth units within HHS. The head of each of the program units within the department explained the policy issues facing that agency and how the budget requested would improve the health and well-being of the nation. In the past, the agency heads often came to the BRB as supplicants, requesting expenditure authority that may or may not have been approved by the BRB and the secretary. This was the first stage of a very complex process, moving from the BRB to the secretary and then to OMB. The "pass-back" from OMB could then be appealed by the secretary, first to the OMB director and then to the president. That was the budget that eventually was presented to the Congress. If a program unit did not receive its request, it was common for the agency (or its constituency) to develop an end-run strategy, working around the secretary and advocating increases in the budget in other decision venues.

The process that was put in place by then secretary Shalala was built around her acknowledgment that the department is a highly decentralized and diverse organization. She was comfortable serving as an advocate for the program units, supporting their agendas, and relying on personal relationships and policy discussion to transmit her own perspective. Thus the BRB's approach changed during the eight years of her tenure (1993–2001), moving away from a centralized control strategy to one in which the Office of the Secretary acknowledged the need for autonomy and discretion within the program units.[28]

At the same time, however, the BRB meetings were organized to help program units construct their budgets in an effective manner, emphasizing themes or specific initiatives highlighted by the secretary. The staff work for the meetings was done by the Budget Office within the Office of the ASMB. The staff members in that office were organized to parallel the structure of the department. Although the Office of the ASMB tried not to be overly directive in its guidance and to give program budget managers some freedom in how they develop their justifications, it found that such freedom sometimes resulted in inconsistencies in the presentation of information.

The BRB helped to define the issues in the budget and through discussion assisted the program units in determining what aspects of the request should be emphasized as the budget was presented to the secretary. The heads of the operating programs were queried about their requests and asked to indicate how those requests meshed with the secretary's initiatives. Representatives of program units other than the one presenting its budget were encouraged to sit in on these presentations. When specific elements were to be included in the budget documents—such as the Annual Performance Plans required by the Government Performance and Results Act—those elements were also discussed in the presentations. In calendar year 2000, the members of the BRB spent more than sixty hours reviewing the agency budget requests. The discussions that took place during the BRB sessions did not result in a collective recommendation; rather, they involved an exchange of information between participants.

Later in the summer the budgets were presented to the secretary and the deputy secretary in a setting that included all the senior staff within the department. All the agencies had an opportunity to review each other's budgets and to comment on areas that were of shared interest. The program unit heads were expected to sit in on each other's presentation to understand the activities of the department as a whole. When these presentations were concluded, all these individuals were asked to prepare a budget for the entire department by voting on allocations—an exercise that emphasized the importance of looking at the submission from the perspective of the secretary. This process gave them some sense of the competing values that characterize the programs in the department and allowed them to develop a sensitivity to the overwhelming demands on the budget that would finally emerge from the department. The secretary imposed a constraint of an overall budget amount and senior staff members made their recommendations within this constraint. Not everything that was requested by the program units appeared in the final budget.

The secretary had four primary sources of inputs to inform her budget decisions: the briefing materials provided by the ASMB's staff, the program presentations at the secretary's meetings, the results of the ballot vote, and the ASMB's recommendations on aggregate budget levels. The final budget represented a melding of the secretary's priorities and program requests from the agencies. This approach minimized the conflict between programs that operated with limited resources. Although cuts were frequently recommended by OMB, in a number of instances the secretary was successful in appealing them to the OMB director or to the president. The unified position within the department was believed to contribute to this success. As such, budget conflict rarely occurred within the department, and a unified position was submitted to OMB. The transparency of the process minimized the practice of program agencies end-running to OMB. At least in some cases, the battle was moved from inside the department to the Executive Office of the President.

Shared Perspectives and a Common Language: The Government Performance and Results Act

After the passage of the Government Performance and Results Act in 1993, the HHS response to the requirements of the legislation was found within the separate program units within the department. This strategy acknowledged the size and decentralized nature of the department. Although charged with the implementation of approximately 300 programs, the size and disparate functions of these programs lent themselves to a decentralized approach to program management and performance measurement.

The specific requirements of the legislation did not go into effect until 1997, but several of the HHS program agencies decided to devise pilot projects (a possibility included in the law) that might serve as demonstrations or examples for others. However, limited attention was paid to these pilot efforts within other parts of the department because the two major requirements of the legislation—a five-year strategic plan and annual performance plans—were not immediate demands.

In 1996 work began seriously on the HHS strategic plan, led by the Office of the Assistant Secretary for Planning and Evaluation. Although a staff-level work group had been formed in early 1994 to develop a department-wide plan and provide technical assistance to the program units as they developed their own plans, these efforts were disrupted by the health care reform initiative and reinvention activities. The guidelines that had been established for that staff-level work group called for a two-part plan—a department-wide part with broad, crosscutting goals and objectives and agency-specific plans to supplement the crosscutting goals.

In the fall of 1996 concerns were expressed about the strategic plan that was emerging through this process. Its critics argued that the plan lacked vision and a strategic focus. The two-level approach was thought to create multiple layers and large numbers of goals, objectives, and strategies that were uncoordinated, duplicative, and did not flow from one another. It was described as the product of a staff-level process, resulting in goals, objectives, and strategies that satisfy major program and constituent interests but fail to articulate a vision or priorities. As a result of these criticisms, the secretary and deputy secretary decided that a document would be written by a few top staffers in ASPE and circulated within the department before it became final. Thus a bottom-up approach was replaced by a document developed in a top-down fashion.

Although this document did present a picture of a unified department, held together by six overarching goals, the strategic plan did not easily fit into the fragmented decision-making structure that is a part of the HHS reality. Both appropriation and authorizing committees in Congress focus on specific program areas, not on broad goals. Even the staff of the Office of Management and Budget only scrutinizes specific elements of the department's programs because separate budget examiners have responsibility for specific program areas. And the approach did not seem consistent with the management approach taken by the secretary and deputy secretary.

In part in reaction to the more centralized ASPE process, the Office of the Assistant Secretary for Management and Budget—the unit within the Office of the Secretary that was given responsibility for the development of the annual performance plans required by GPRA—developed a strategy that emphasized the unique nature of the individual HHS program components. Because the performance plans were attached to the budget submissions, their development was clearly a bottom-up process.

During the first several years of the process, the role of the ASMB was that of a gentle facilitator who attempted to provide opportunities for representatives of program units to raise questions and discuss their experiences. The annual performance plans that were devised were very different from one another. Although most of the program units made some reference to the themes established by the strategic plan, their performance plans—as did the budgets—emphasized quite diverse goals and objectives.

The deliberations within the congressional appropriations process did not indicate that members of Congress were focused on the problems that stemmed from the diversity of these documents, but there was strong criticism of the HHS submissions by the General Accounting Office and by the Republican congressional leadership. The model of decision making that was employed by these critics assumed that HHS was managed as a centralized command and control department. Although this model was not realistic for a department of the size and scope of HHS (nor did it comport with the secretary's personal approach), there was a danger that the criticism of the GPRA submissions could cause problems for the department.

Thus the staff of the ASMB was faced with a dilemma: how could it respect the diversity and autonomy of the program units and, at the same time, find ways to address the critics who sought a unified, single document? In addition, there clearly was a range of GPRA-related competencies within the department and it would be useful for program unit staff to find ways to learn from one another.

The strategy that was employed within the ASMB contained several aspects. The ASMB staff developed a performance plan summary document that did provide a more unified picture of the department. It focused on the linkage between program unit goals and objectives and departmental initiatives and the HHS strategic plan. It highlighted crosscutting areas, drawing on the individual performance plans to illustrate shared areas. It set out the HHS approach to performance measurement and the close relationship between the department's budget development process and the GPRA performance plans.

In addition, the ASMB staff held a series of conference calls that provided an opportunity for program unit staff to discuss issues, share experiences, and develop a collegial (almost collective) approach to the task. These calls (and some face-to-face meetings) were constructed to provide methods of active rather than passive involvement in the process.

Finally, the ASMB staff worked closely with a subgroup of the GPRA program unit staff to develop a standardized format that all program components agreed to use for their 2001 performance plans and their 1999 performance reports. This format established a consistent "order of presentation" of information required by the law and OMB for performance plans and reports. Significant flexibility remained, however, to ensure that the units were able to tailor their performance plans and reports to meet their individual needs. Some components chose to present certain types of performance information at the agency level; others chose to present information at the program or goal levels. For the reader who was required to assess all the HHS performance plans, this shared format painted a picture of some level of consistency across the program units and did make the job of reading the documents somewhat easier.

The changes that took place during the Clinton administration clearly shifted the roles of several of the units within the Office of the Secretary. Perhaps the major change came in the Office of the Assistant Secretary for Planning and Evaluation, originally created in 1965 to serve as the principal adviser to the secretary and responsible for policy coordination, legislative development, strategic planning, policy research and evaluation, and economic analyses.[29] That office was created at a time when the secretary of the department sought a mechanism to provide a way to control what were viewed as very separate entities within what was then HEW. The policy analysis office was responsive only to the secretary's agenda (not to the program units) and provided a way for the cabinet official to find ways to link and control the autonomous units in the department. This was particularly important during an era of creation of new policies, when decisions taken in one unit might have implications for the work in another. ASPE also provided an analytic capability to look beyond the confines of the department and to indicate areas where other federal agencies might be affected by (or affect) HHS programs. But when HHS was approached as a decentralized organization, ASPE became much less visible and less attached to a general management strategy. It did play a leading role in several specific policy areas (for example, health, privacy, health disparities, and bioterrorism) but did not have an impact on overall management.

The other unit that experienced significant change was the Office of the Assistant Secretary for Management and Budget. At one level, the ASMB office that operated during the Clinton administration had a wider span of power than its predecessors. It was not until midway through the first Clinton term that the management function was combined with the human resources responsibility as well as some of the financial management activities. But at the same time, the budget role—perhaps the most important role of ASMB—took on new meaning as more authority was delegated to the program units within the department. This changed the dynamics of the budget process, but it did not always result in major differences in final budget outcomes. In the past, it was not uncommon for program units that received large budget cuts at the department level to find ways to use constituency groups and congressional contacts to move toward their original budget requests.

SOURCES OF OVERSIGHT

Although much of the information that is available to a cabinet secretary comes directly from the program offices within a department, other sources of intelligence are also available. Some of that information is developed inside the agency through offices that are responsible for oversight. Still other aspects of that information come from outside the organization, particularly from the GAO, the analytic unit responsible to Congress that regularly assesses the performance of federal programs. In addition, a cabinet official has access to the analytical work of the Office of Inspector General (OIG), which includes units largely established by the Inspector General Act of 1978 and provides information both to the agency and to Congress about agency performance.[30]

Oversight Inside the Department

The Office of Finance, located inside the Office of the Assistant Secretary for Management and Budget, serves as the internal source of information for financial management inside HHS. This office manages and directs HHS implementation of major financial management legislation, including the Chief Financial Officers Act of 1990 (CFO Act), the Government Management Reform Act of 1994 (GMRA), the Prompt Payment Act, the Cash Management Improvement Act (CMIA), and the Debt Collection Improvement Act of 1996, among others.

Because HHS had net outlays of $359.7 billion in fiscal year 1999 (21.1 percent of the federal budget), it has enormous responsibility for financial accountability. HHS is a key player in the government-wide financial statement audit, which was prepared for the first time for fiscal year 1997. In addition, the Office of Finance produces a yearly accountability report that highlights the importance of strong financial management.

Working with the program offices, the Office of Finance has responsibility for initiatives such as developing and implementing accounting and financial policies, systems, and reports; resolving financial statement audit findings; implementing financial and program performance measurement; making prompt payments; budget execution; improving reliability of financial information; developing and coordinating policy for debt collection; implementing all financial management legislation; and integrating all the financial management initiatives. These data provide a cabinet official with appropriate information that will identify problems in financial management within the department.

Oversight Outside the Department

Given the size of the HHS budget and the areas of dispute around its programs, it is not surprising that the General Accounting Office has undertaken a series of reports about the performance and accountability challenges facing the department. Although some GAO reports are developed in response to specific congressional requests, others are attempts to step back and provide an assessment of executive-branch performance.

In January 2001 the GAO issued a series of reports entitled *Performance and Accountability Series: Major Management Challenges and Program Risks.* Separate reports on twenty-one agencies were released; the HHS report was one of the most complex of the submissions.[31] In its introduction to the report, the GAO wrote:

> The Department of Health and Human Services (HHS), with a $376-billion budget, presents one of the more massive and complex management and program-related challenges in the federal government. The federal health and social programs it oversees tangibly affect the lives and well-being of virtually all Americans and encompass some of the most costly issues facing the nation.[32]

Six challenges were identified in this report; many of them focused on areas that had received congressional attention in the recent past:

- Provide current and future generations with a well-designed and well-administered Medicare program.
- Better safeguard the integrity of the Medicare program.
- Improve oversight of nursing homes so that residents receive quality care.
- Ensure the safety and efficacy of medical products.
- Enhance the economic independence and well-being of children and families.

This report builds on earlier studies undertaken by the GAO. Three of the areas of concern focus on programs found within the Centers for Medicare and Medicaid Services (CMS), especially the Medicare program. Reports such as these provide an important source of information to a cabinet secretary about the issues that are likely to be on the agenda of various members of Congress, raised during both the appropriations and the authorization processes.

Oversight Both Inside and Outside the Department

The HHS Office of Inspector General was created in 1976, one of the earliest such offices in the federal government. The office was originally designed to promote "economy, efficiency, and effectiveness" in the department and "to prevent and detect fraud and abuse" in its programs.[33] Although the office was originally designed largely as an investigative and audit unit, by the late 1970s an evaluation and inspections unit was created that focused on short-term program analyses. This office was established during the Carter administration by then-secretary Joseph Califano, who wanted information that measured the effectiveness of service delivery independently of those data produced by the program units.[34] Originally called the Service Delivery Assessment Program and placed in the Office of the Assistant Secretary for Planning and Evaluation, the activity was moved to the OIG in 1977.

Because of its dual responsibilities (reporting both to the department and to Congress), over the years the OIG has been able to provide information to both of its clients. In 1990, for example, the HHS inspector general testified twenty-three times before Congress.[35] At other times the OIG has been an important source of advice to the secretary. That advice comes in various forms: through specific reports about individual programs and through publications that review a range of recommendations. For example, the OIG issues something that it calls the "Red Book"—a compendium of cost-saving recommendations that have not been fully implemented. These recommendations tend to focus on programs within the HCFA, within other parts of the public health agencies, the ACF, and the AoA. For each recommendation, the current law is summarized, the reason is given why action is needed, the estimated savings that would result from taking the recommended action is given, and the status of actions taken is put forth. In addition, the type of action needed (legislative, regulatory, or other administrative) is indicated.

The savings estimates for these unimplemented recommendations are updated from time to time to reflect more current data as they become available. These estimates have varying levels of precision, and the actual savings to be achieved depend on the specific legislative, regulatory, or administrative action taken. However, the estimates provide a general indication of the magnitude of savings possible.

The OIG can also have an impact on the design of policies and programs within the department. For example, during the late 1990s the OIG focused on the procedures that were used to protect human subjects in research projects sponsored by the federal government (largely the NIH and the FDA). The instrumentality for implementing these policies is the Institutional Review Board (IRB). These bodies are established and operated by universities, hospitals, and other institutions that receive research awards from the federal government or other sponsors. They are responsible for reviewing proposed research protocols and informed consent statements before subjects are recruited and clinical research begins as well as for continuing oversight of the projects throughout their life cycle.

Three reports were issued in 1998 by the OIG, pointing to some of the problems associated with protection of human subjects and highlighting the demands and pressures on the IRBs that made it difficult for them to carry out their role. The OIG asserted that it was time for a fundamental reexamination and reengineering of the HHS oversight process in this area. These reports contributed to a major modification of the HHS policy on human subject protection, in part spurred on by the death of a young man in an experimental gene transplant effort at the University of Pennsylvania.

CONCLUSION

Each of the areas discussed in this chapter—organization structure; personnel issues; the role of the Office of the Secretary; and mechanisms for internal oversight—do require attention from the secretary. But as the discussion indicated, each of them is surrounded by an environment of turbulence and change. Few of the programs within the department can be treated as simply internal management challenges. Rather, they require the secretary and the top staff to give attention to internal management functions within the context of constantly shifting political and social forces. They demand that the secretary lead, not simply manage.

Raymond Wilson realizes that he does need functions and units within the Office of the Secretary that allow him to respond to issues that take on crisis proportions or require action across program lines. At the same time, he knows that the day-to-day operations of the department take place within the separate program units. He doesn't want to be perceived as a micro-manager by the staff, whom he trusts and has selected in consultation with the White House and Congress. Yet he knows that some programs are more difficult to implement than others and are vulnerable to a variety of both political and managerial challenges. As a result of his preparation for the hearings, Wilson understands that he will need to create an information system that both give him regular feedback on the activities of the program units and, as well, provide some independent data on the performance of program units. Although he chose not to adopt a highly centralized, control orientation to management, he knows that he needs to keep abreast of what is happening within his portfolio.

Notes

1. Graham T. Allison, "Public and Private Management: Are They Fundamentally Alike in All Unimportant Respects?" in *Classics of Public Administration,* 3d ed., ed. Jay M. Shafritz and Albert C. Hyde (Belmont, Calif.: Wadsworth, 1992), 457.

2. Selma Mushkin, quoted in ibid., 458.

3. Luther Gulick and Lyndall Urwick, quoted in ibid., 459–460.

4. Mark H. Moore, *Creating Public Value: Strategic Management in Government* (Cambridge: Harvard University Press, 1995), 10.

5. Robert B. Reich, *Public Management in a Democratic Society* (Englewood Cliffs, N.J.: Prentice Hall, 1990), 4, 5–8.

6. W. Michael Blumenthal, "Candid Reflections of a Businessman in Washington," *Fortune,* January 29, 1979, 39, 48.

7. Moore, *Creating Public Value,* 299.

8. Kevin M. Bacon and Mark A. Abramson, *Reflections from the Top: Management Advice from Government CEOs* (Arlington, Va.: PricewaterhouseCoopers [circa 1996]), 3.

9. James G. March and Johan P. Olsen describe reorganization as "a domain of rhetoric, trading, problematic attention, and symbolic action." March and Olsen, "Organizing Political Life: What Administrative Reorganization Tells Us About Government," *American Political Science Review* 77 (1983): 291.

10. David Osborne and Ted Gaebler, *Reinventing Government: How the Entrepreneurial Spirit Is Transforming the Public Sector* (Reading, Mass.: Addison-Wesley, 1992).

11. Joseph A. Califano Jr., *Governing America: An Insider's Report from the White House and the Cabinet* (New York: Simon and Schuster, 1981), 441.

12. Donna E. Shalala, "Are Large Public Organizations Manageable?" *Public Administration Review* 58 (July–August 1998): 285.

13. Albert Gore, *From Red Tape to Result: Creating a Government That Works Better and Costs Less* (known as the Gore report), report of the National Performance Review (Washington, D.C.: Government Printing Office, 1993).

14. See discussion in Beryl A. Radin, *Managing Decentralized Departments: The Case of the U.S. Department of Health and Human Services,* Grant Report, PricewaterhouseCoopers Endowment for the Business of Government, October 1999.

15. Cited in Beryl A. Radin and Willis D. Hawley, *The Politics of Reorganization: Creating the U.S. Department of Education* (New York: Pergamon Press, 1988), 32.

16. See discussion in Rufus E. Miles Jr., *The Department of HEW* (New York: Praeger, 1974), 66.

17. See discussion in James W. Fesler and Donald F. Kettl, *The Politics of the Administrative Process,* 2d ed. (Chatham, N.J.: Chatham House, 1996), 115.

18. See discussion in Mark R. Yessian, "The Generalist Perspective in the HEW Bureaucracy: An Account from the Field," *Public Administration Review 40* (March–April 1980).

19. Blumenthal, "Candid Reflections of a Businessman in Washington."

20. Fesler and Kettl, *The Politics of the Administrative Process,* 143.

21. Ibid., 144.

22. On the criticism, see, for example, Paul C. Light, *Thickening Government: Federal Hierarchy and the Diffusion of Accountability* (Washington, D.C.: Brookings Institution, 1995), and what is known as the Volker Commission Report, *Rebuilding the Public Service,* National Commission on the Public Service, GAO 1989. On

unproductive conflict, see Hugh Heclo, *A Government of Strangers: Executive Politics in Washington* (Washington, D.C.: Brookings Institution, 1977).

23. Shalala, "Are Large Public Organizations Manageable?" 286.

24. Califano, *Governing America,* 46.

25. U.S. General Accounting Office, *Management of HHS: Using the Office of the Secretary to Enhance Departmental Effectiveness,* report to Congress, GAO HRD-90-54, February 1990, 3.

26. Ibid.

27. See Radin, *The Challenge of Managing Across Boundaries: The Case of the Office of the Secretary in the U.S. Department of Health and Human Services,* Grant Report, PricewaterhouseCoopers Endowment for the Business of Government, November 2000.

28. See Radin, *Managing Decentralized Departments,* 16–17, for a partial discussion of these issues.

29. A profile of this office is found in Beryl A. Radin, *Beyond Machiavelli: Policy Analysis Comes of Age* (Washington, D.C.: Georgetown University Press, 2000), 57–61.

30. There are significant variations in the assessment of effectiveness of the Offices of Inspector General. Paul C. Light has pointed out the limits of this office in *Monitoring Government: Inspectors General and the Search for Accountability* (Washington, D.C.: Brookings Institution, 1993).

31. U.S. General Accounting Office *Major Management Challenges and Program Risk, Department of Health and Human Services,* GAO-01-247, January 2001.

32. Ibid., 6.

33. See Penny R. Thompson and Mark R. Yessian, "Policy Analysis in the Office of Inspector General, U.S. Department of Health and Human Services," in *Organizations for Policy Analysis: Helping Government Think,* ed. Carol H. Weiss (Newbury Park, Calif.: Sage Publications, 1992), 161–180.

34. Califano, *Governing America,* 46.

35. Cited in Light, *Thickening Government,* 56.

7

Dealing with the Public

ALTHOUGH he is focused on his Senate confirmation hearings, Raymond Wilson is beginning to appreciate how difficult it will be to communicate the dimensions of his coming job to the many publics that are interested in HHS programs. The multiple perspectives that were found just within the membership of the two Senate committees hearing his nomination have given him a glimpse of the world beyond confirmation. He not only has to deal with the accountability demands made by others but he recognizes that he will have to learn to communicate both the complexity of the role and his technical grasp of the issues before him to many different audiences.

His relationship with the various publics surrounding HHS also affect the ability of the department to get information from those publics. His predecessors told him that one of the most annoying aspects of the job came when the *Washington Post* or the *New York Times* gave them the first information about an interest group taking a position on an issue facing the department. Several of the former secretaries said they felt they were ambushed by those stories. Sometimes the explanation for this involved poor communication within the department. More frequently it occurred because the department did not have ongoing, regular relationships with those groups, and those groups did not think to inform the secretary about their positions before they were released to the press.

THIS CHAPTER sketches some of the ways that HHS deals with the public. I describe the units within the department that have special responsibilities in this area—the Office of the Assistant Secretary for Public Affairs, the Office of the Assistant Secretary for Legislation, and the Office of Intergovernmental Affairs. I also outline the mechanisms that are available to the department to listen to individuals with an interest in the department's policies and programs, particularly the advisory committees operating within the agency. Finally, I discuss the opportunities that are available to HHS to tell its story or, as some would characterize it, to make its case, particularly the bully pulpit available to the secretary through speeches and other public appearances.

As the previous chapters have indicated, an HHS secretary has to find a way to balance the demands of competing expectations. Each set of expectations is attached to the institutions, structures, and processes that are part of the world of a cabinet official. Although turbulent and constantly changing, at least these expectations can be located in fairly well defined venues.

But dealing with the public is much more amorphous. The mechanisms that are available to a cabinet official to make his or her case to the public are neither subject to official scrutiny nor in the orbit of formal influence or control. In fact, many of these mechanisms involve the various press media that are protected by constitutional norms of free speech. Because there are few ways that the cabinet secretary can deal directly with the public as a whole, the press often becomes a surrogate for viewing public opinion or attempting to influence it. Although polls, focus groups, and other public opinion techniques can be useful, they have limited ability to influence the details of agency decision making.

As in many other instances, dealing with the public calls for a cabinet official to be responsive to issues that are raised by the public, often in newspapers or television, and, at the same time, to find ways to command public attention in a way that facilitates public approval of the departmental agenda. John Kingdon has noted that the media are important to the development of public opinion and—as a result—to the acceptance or rejection of a policy agenda.[1] The media alone cannot place an issue on the policy agenda, but their ability to give more or less attention to that issue can create a set of pressures that require the attention of a top government official. Whether or not an issue has high priority in the cabinet official's agenda, it can be pushed aside by a front-page story in the *Washington Post* or the *New York Times* on another question.

Kingdon notes that the media do have the ability to affect the government policy agenda in several ways. First, it acts as a communicator within a policy community. Second, it has the ability to magnify movements that have already started elsewhere. And third, it affects some of the participants in the process who believe that media attention is the same as public concern.[2]

In addition to focusing on the press, a cabinet-level department head also deals with the public in a variety of modes. A cabinet secretary must find methods that provide input from various groups affected by the policies and programs of the department and also offer opportunities to make the agency's case to those groups as well as to others with an interest in agency programs and policies.

As John Trattner has written, the nature of dealing with the media offers a real challenge to federal agency leaders. He suggests several strategies. First, the agency should find creative ways to attract positive coverage and to tell its story both honestly and factually. Second, an agency needs to know how to deal with bad news to minimize its impact. Third, an agency has to respect the reality of journalists; they are driven by deadlines and competition. And fourth, agencies need to develop productive working relationships with journalists, minimizing the natural suspicion that is present on both sides.[3]

HHS STAFF OFFICES

Three offices within the Office of the Secretary have had special responsibilities for dealing with the public. These include the Office of the Assistant Secretary for Public Affairs, the Office of the Assistant Secretary for Legislation, and the Office of Intergovernmental Affairs.

The Office of the Assistant Secretary for Public Affairs

This office attempts to balance two related responsibilities: to serve the direct public communication needs of the secretary and, at the same time, to provide oversight for the extensive public affairs activities that take place throughout the department. During Donna Shalala's terms in office, ASPA worked closely with the public affairs staff members found in each of the program units within HHS to deal with this latter responsibility. Other secretaries have centralized the function within the Office of the Secretary. During the Shalala years, each program unit had its own press and public affairs office and many subagencies also had their own press and public affairs staff.

When operating in a decentralized system, this staff office not only helps to develop and convey a sense of the department's plans and priorities but it also keeps track of the details of these efforts that frequently generate areas of controversy. It also helps to identify the best opportunities for the secretary to mark the achievements of the organization and to announce key findings of HHS programs. ASPA not only communicated these efforts outside of the department but also sought to assist in ensuring that the secretary's priorities were understood and reinforced by the agencies within the department's umbrella. Both the external and internal strategies call on ASPA to attempt to convey a coherent picture of the department.

ASPA provided a full range of public affairs tools to serve the secretary's direct public communication needs, including media liaison, speechwriting, briefing background, and production of broadcast and Internet materials. Overseeing public affairs activities through the rest of the department means that the office usually develops a clearance process, asking each of the program public affairs offices to ensure that the Office of the Secretary is aware of program relationships with the press.

The nature of the issues within the HHS portfolio creates constant attention by the media to the policies and programs within the department. Print journalists from papers such as the *New York Times* and the *Washington Post* have regular assignments in areas such as health and welfare. Television news programs such as *60 Minutes* have frequently developed special segments on such problems as Medicare fraud. As a result of the press attention, top staff in ASPA play important roles as advisers to the secretary during the policy development process. If the issue is expected to be controversial, it is important to raise the anticipated media response during that process. Frequently assistant secretaries have become close and trusted advisers to the secretary in these circumstances, especially when the public affairs official comes to the department with past relationships with the media.

During the Shalala years, ASPA operated through several divisions. The news division acted as the central HHS press office, handling media requests, clearing all press releases and interviews, and managing news issues that cut across program areas. This division produced a daily service of news clippings that dealt with HHS staff and programs. The communication division supported the secretary's TV and radio appearances and managed the department's own TV studio. It provided special outreach to minority and specialty media. The speechwriting division produced speeches and articles for the secretary and deputy secretary. Finally, the Freedom of Information division responded to requests for information made to the Office of the Secretary and coordinated policies and activities of similar offices within the program units.

The Office of the Assistant Secretary for Legislation

This office has been responsible for the development and implementation of the department's legislative agenda and also serves as the HHS liaison with members of Congress, their staffs, and congressional committees with jurisdiction over HHS programs. The Office of the ASL provides advice to the secretary on all matters dealing with legislation; it informs members of Congress about the department's priorities, views on pending legislation, policy decisions, and awards of grants and contracts.

ASL supports the HHS legislative agenda in a number of ways. It works closely with the White House and OMB to advise Congress about presidential initiatives and priorities in Congress. It coordinates testimony of the secretary and other HHS officials before Congress, secretarial meetings with members, and invitations from Congress for the secretary to speak before various groups. It responds to routine congressional inquiries on behalf of constituents and notifies congressional offices of grant awards made by HHS agencies. It also advises the secretary and other senior officials concerning congressional investigations and oversight issues affecting department programs; and it manages the confirmation process for the secretary and the seventeen other presidential appointees who must be confirmed by the Senate.

In addition, ASL works closely with HHS program agency legislation offices to prepare witnesses and testimony for hearings (except appropriations committee hearings that are the responsibility of the assistant secretary for management and budget); develops policies, clears legislative language, and transmits proposed legislation to the Congress; conducts congressional briefings on department programs and initiatives; and provides technical assistance on draft and pending legislation; develops, clears, and transmits administration positions to Congress on pending legislation; and provides technical assistance to members and their staffs during committee mark-up of bills and in preparation for floor actions.

ASL deals with a wide range of congressional committees that have jurisdiction over HHS programs. These include the following House committees: the Committee on Commerce (with jurisdiction over Medicare, Medicaid, child health insurance, and all programs of the public health agencies); the Committee on Education and the Workforce (jurisdiction over Head Start, programs for older Americans, child care, and other human services discretionary programs); the Committee on the Judiciary (jurisdiction over the violence against women and immigration programs); the Committee on Ways and Means (jurisdiction over parts of Medicare and entitlement programs such as child welfare, foster care, and adoption assistance); and the Committee on Resources (joint jurisdiction with the Commerce Committee over the Indian Health Service).

A similar range of committees is found in the Senate: the Committee on Finance (jurisdiction for Medicare, Medicaid, child health insurance, and the same programs covered by the House Ways and Means Committee); the Committee on Health, Education, Labor, and Pensions (jurisdiction for all public health agency programs except IHS and the same human service discretionary programs as the House Education and Workforce Committee); the Committee on Indian Affairs (jurisdiction over IHS and other Native American programs); and the Committee on Judiciary (jurisdiction over violence against women and immigration programs).

ASL assists the secretary with the multi-stage confirmation process. The office makes all arrangements for courtesy visits and the hearing, and it devises a strategy for addressing any concerns that arise so that objections may be resolved and the nomination will be sent to the floor with a favorable result. This consists of the following steps: ASL helps manage department briefings for the nominee; the White House formally nominates the candidate; ASL assists with the preparation of required forms, the preparation of the nomination packet, and transmittal of the packet from the White House to the Senate; ASL sets up courtesy visits with Senate leadership, committee members, and Senate staff; the nominee testifies at a hearing before the committee of jurisdiction. ASL responds to questions for the record and other hearing follow-up; the nominee is reported out of the committee with a majority vote; ASL arranges courtesy visits with other key senators; the nomination is cleared for the Senate floor and put on the floor calendar; and the nominee is approved by a majority vote of the Senate.

The Office of Intergovernmental Affairs (IGA)

Over the years, the office that is designed to reach out to the intergovernmental actors who do business with HHS has had various configurations. In most of these configurations the office has had fairly high visibility within the department, reporting to the deputy secretary or directly to the secretary. The office that was created during the Clinton administration was a unit that worked closely with the regional directors and operated out of the Office of the Secretary.

During the Shalala years the primary function of the Office of Intergovernmental Affairs was to ensure that the department considered and incorporated the perspectives of state, local, and tribal governments in the development and implementation of its policies. During the recent past, this office emphasized an intergovernmental consultation process as its chief tool, working with each program element within the department to bring the perspectives of the intergovernmental actors into focus.

The IGA office served as a vehicle not only for hearing the voices of the intergovernmental partners but also for formulating outreach strategies, providing technical assistance, and disseminating information about policies and policy proposals for the department. This office operated as an intermediary between the national organizations that represent states, local governments, and tribes as well as a contact between the department and the individual states, localities, and tribes. The IGA office closely monitored the work of the National Governors' Association, the National Conference of State Legislatures, the U.S. Conference of Mayors, the National League of Cities, the National Association of Counties, and various tribal groups.

During 2000, the IGA office focused on the implementation of the Children's Health Insurance Program (particularly issues related to outreach and enrollment). This office highlighted the implementation of Temporary Assistance for Needy Families (TANF) and Medicaid and the federal role in welfare reform, child care programs, tribal consultation, and issues related to outreach involving public health initiatives, particularly efforts to eliminate racial and ethnic health disparities.

ADVISORY COMMITTEES

Over the years, federal agencies have amassed many committees, boards, commissions, councils, and similar groups to advise officers and agencies in the executive branch. Beginning in 1972 Congress focused its attention on these groups, attempting to establish criteria for creating these units as well as the ground rules for their operation. The enactment of the 1972 Federal Advisory Committee Act (FACA) was intended to keep the number of advisory committees to the minimum. Subsequent amendments were enacted that sought to further define the role and management of these entities and to ensure that Congress was kept informed of their activities.

In 1993 an executive order set out a goal of reducing the number of discretionary advisory committees by at least one-third by the end of fiscal year 1993 and reducing the costs of the committees and the number of committee members at the same time. The GAO found that the number of advisory committees did drop in 1994 but that the costs and the number of committee members actually increased during the same period.[4]

The total number of advisory committees in the federal government was approximately 1,000 in fiscal year 1996. Of that number 243 were found to be in HHS—almost a fourth of the bodies in the entire federal government. Although these committees are distributed across the department, many of them are found within the science agencies. They provide expertise for the NIH and the other science organizations to call on as needed to assist the agency in establishing priorities and making judgments about the quality of submissions for funding through the peer review process. These committees reinforce the autonomy of the science agencies, limiting the ability of the secretary to control their actions through formal and hierarchical methods.

Before implementing the executive order, there were 235 advisory committees just in NIH. And a report of the HHS Office of Inspector General in 1994 found that NIH did not have adequate procedures to detect potential conflicts of interest in its advisory committees.[5]

In 1998 the GAO solicited the views of various committee members and federal agencies on federal advisory committee issues. A high percentage of advisory committee members felt that the membership of their unit was fairly balanced in points of view represented and included a cross section of those directly interested in and affected by the issues. They also found that the agency usually acted in line with the general consensus of the committee.[6]

At the same time, agencies were asked to rate how useful and burdensome they found some of the FACA requirements. More than half of the agencies queried viewed the requirements more or somewhat more useful than burdensome, whereas about 10 percent found them more burdensome than useful.[7] Twenty-six mandated advisory committees were identified by agencies as candidates for termination; of those, eleven were in HHS.[8]

THE DEPARTMENT TELLS ITS STORY

Much of what a cabinet department secretary does in regard to reaching out to various elements of the public is reactive. Whether stories in the printed press, exposés on television, or summons to congressional oversight hearings, the secretary of a department has to be able to respond to external demands. At the same time, however, there are regular opportunities in the normal course of doing the public's business that have the potential to provide opportunities for a secretary to tell his or her own story. This can be done through speeches to various groups throughout the country, appearances on television (especially the Sunday political interview programs), and interviews. Depending on the political construct of the time (for example, whether one political party has control of one or both congressional houses and another has control of the White House), appropriations and authorizing committee hearings may work to the department's advantage or disadvantage.

Perhaps no part of HHS is more skilled in maximizing the opportunities of an advantageous atmosphere than the various program elements in the NIH. NIH directors are often able to focus on specific concerns of committee members and tailor their testimony to meet those interests, especially during the appropriations committee hearings. And stories of scientific discoveries are sometimes presented in a way that suggests the contours of a good mystery story, capturing the imagination of the politicians as they hear the details about the search for cures for various diseases.

Few top department officials go into the congressional hearing room without extensive preparation. Their staff members have usually attempted to predict the types of questions that will be asked and provide their superiors with appropriate answers. Attempts are made to minimize attention to the aspects of programs that are controversial or divisive and, instead, to focus on those elements in programs and policies that transcend partisan, geographical, and population lines. If the cabinet secretary or the top official is new and unknown to the committee members, it may take some time to develop a trust relationship between those members and their staff and the agency head. When the agency head has appeared before the committee earlier (and congressional staff has had access to the agency between appearances), there is less of a tendency for the members to be on the attack.

By the time Donna Shalala completed her eight-year term as a cabinet secretary, her relationship with members of Congress was cordial and warm, despite the partisan differences between the two branches of government. Part of this was a result of her longevity in the role, but perhaps more important was her commitment to be available and responsive to all members of Congress. As a result, the hearing appearances were not usually characterized by an adversarial tone.

Similarly, the secretary can use the opportunity created by the release of reports to make a case for the administration's policies and positions. Some of the reports are required through legislation, others emerge from studies that were accomplished within the relevant agency. The following are some of the reports released in 2000 within HHS.

- *Mental Health: A Report of the Surgeon General.* HHS released the first surgeon general's report on mental health. The report focuses on issues such as the connection between mental health and physical health; barriers to receiving mental health treatment; the specific mental health issues of children, adults, and the elderly; and areas in which further research and analysis are necessary to understand the impact of mental health issues on special populations, such as racial and ethnic groups and people with disabilities.
- *Patterns of Alcohol Use Among Adolescents and Associations with Emotional and Behavioral Problems.* In March the Substance Abuse and Mental Health Services Administration released a report showing a strong relationship between alcohol use among youth and emotional and behavioral problems, including fighting, driving under the influence of alcohol or drugs, skipping school, and feeling depressed. This report is based on a sample of 18,000 adolescents who participated in SAMHSA's 1994, 1995, and 1996 National Household Surveys on Drug Abuse.
- *Declines in Teenage Birth Rates, 1991–98: Update of National and State Trends.* HHS announced the availability of this report, which indicates a continuing decline in birth rates for adolescents ages fifteen through eighteen.
- *Substance Abuse in Popular Movies and Music Study.* The White House Office of National Drug Control Policy (ONDCP) and the Substance Abuse and Mental Health Services Administration released the results of this study, which examined the amount of illicit drug, alcohol, and tobacco use depicted in popular movies and music. The study was conducted to establish a basis for dialog and collaboration between substance abuse prevention professionals and the entertainment industry and to encourage parents to be informed about the content of music and movies their children are listening to and watching.

Studies are also released that provide a way for the department to communicate its perspective to the public. Several studies illustrate this:

- *The Youth Risk Behavior Surveillance System/Youth Risk Behavior Survey.* The CDC conducts this biennial survey of students in grades nine through twelve to assess the prevalence of health risk behaviors among high school students. Survey topics include injury-related behaviors, tobacco use, alcohol and other drug use, sexual behaviors, physical activity, and dietary behaviors.

- *Estimates of U.S. Children Exposed to Alcohol Abuse and Dependence in the Family.* The National Institute on Alcohol Abuse and Alcoholism (NIAAA), National Institutes of Health announced the release of this study in the January 2000 issue of the *American Journal of Public Health.* It reported that approximately one in four U.S. children (19 million children, or 28.6 percent of children from birth to seventeen years of age) is exposed at some time before age eighteen to familial alcohol dependence, alcohol abuse, or both.
- *Add Health: A National Longitudinal Study of Adolescent Health.* The National Institute of Child Health and Human Development, the National Institutes of Health, and seventeen other federal agencies funded this landmark study. The study was done to measure the impact of social environment on adolescent health and examine the general health and well-being of adolescents. Study topics included adolescent health and health-affecting behaviors; influences on adolescent health such as families, friends, and peers; romantic relationships; schools; neighborhoods; and communities. Data were collected on adolescents in grades nine through twelve during the first year of the study in 1994–1995.
- *Monitoring the Future Survey.* The National Institute on Drug Abuse (NIDA) annually monitors young people to determine their lifetime, past-year, past-month, and daily use of drugs, alcohol, cigarettes, and smokeless tobacco. According to the results of the twenty-fifth annual survey, overall illicit drug use among youth in 1999 remained unchanged from 1998. This marked the third consecutive year that adolescent substance abuse declined or stayed level. More than 45,000 eighth, tenth, and twelfth graders in 433 schools across the country were surveyed. The survey, conducted by the University of Michigan's Institute for Social Research with funding from NIDA was released by HHS.

CONCLUSION

Communicating with the public either directly or through media institutions is an important task for an HHS secretary. As such, the jobs (particularly the ASPA job) within the department that deal with the public are among the most important tasks within the Office of the Secretary. The image that is produced of agency programs or staff competencies by external actors can dramatically affect the success or failure of a cabinet secretary's agenda and tenure. This image is closely tied to the various accountability demands that are made on a cabinet secretary. As indicated in this chapter, many processes and institutions are available to the secretary as well as to those outside the department that have an impact on that image. But, like other aspects of the cabinet secretary's life, it is difficult to predict the direction of that image and the way the public will perceive the work of HHS.

Notes

1. John W. Kingdon, *Agendas, Alternatives, and Public Policies,* 2d ed. (New York: HarperCollins, 1995), 57–59.

2. Ibid., 59–60.

3. John H. Trattner, *The 2000 Prune Book: How to Succeed in Washington's Top Jobs* (Washington, D.C.: Brookings Institution), 38–47.

4. General Accounting Office, *Federal Advisory Committee Act: Overview of Advisory Committees Since 1993,* testimony of L. Nye Stevens before the Subcommittee on Government Management, Information, and Technology, House Committee on Government Reform and Oversight, GAO/T-GGD-98-24, November 5, 1997.

5. Office of Inspector General, HHS, *Review of the National Institutes of Health's Controls over Advisory Committees' Potential Conflicts of Interest,* audit, A-15-93, 00020, March 23, 1994.

6. General Accounting Office, *Federal Advisory Committee Act: Advisory Committee Process Appears to Be Working, but Some Concerns Exist,* testimony of L. Nye Stevens before the Subcommittee on Government Management, Information, and Technology, House Committee on Government Reform and Oversight, GAO/T-GGD-98-163, July 14, 1998.

7. Ibid., 7.

8. U.S. General Accounting Office, *Federal Advisory Committee Act: Views of Committee Members and Agencies on Federal Advisory Committee Issues,* GAO/GGD-98–147, July 9, 1998.

Advice to a New
HHS Secretary

THIS BOOK is an attempt to paint a picture of the complex web of accountability demands that make up the world of a cabinet secretary. In it I have sought to show how the American political system makes the job of a cabinet official incredibly demanding, particularly an official charged with managing a vast empire such as HHS.

We have seen that multiple programs and functions interact with the fragmented institutions of governance. Technical concerns are often entwined with political realities. The lives of citizens are directly affected by what seem to be narrow administrative decisions. A cabinet secretary is required to move beyond the formal legal, fiscal, and institutional requirements of the position and to confront emergent and often unpredictable issues, perceptions, and crises.

Study of these attributes of office provides a perspective on accountability that moves far beyond the traditional perspective on the topic. Conflict, constant change, and diversity mean that there are no firm rules because what works in one situation is not effective in another. A cabinet secretary is likely to be effective when he or she is able to identify a set of questions; rarely can an official move into the position with firm answers or a detailed road map.

The questions that Raymond Wilson set forth in preparing for his confirmation hearings provide a check list and a sense of the general contours of a cabinet position. Cabinet secretaries must deal with overall questions of strategy, devise various approaches to the multiple subcultures and program designs within a department, concern themselves with the players and processes involved in political relationships, and find the appropriate balance between centralized and decentralized functions within the department. At the same time, he or she cannot forget the purpose of public organizations—to provide services to the American citizenry. The cabinet official is placed in a unique leadership role.

Yet much of what has been written about leadership of organizations in either the public or the private sector suggests behavior that verges on the heroic. If

Raymond Wilson followed the advice of these writers and advisers, he would believe that it was important to come to his cabinet position with a vision of what is
important to him and what he can do to imprint his personality on that organization and make sure that his vision is central and clearly articulated to others in
the organization. Former navy secretary Richard Danzig characterized this heroic
approach as follows:

> Think of three things that the organization wouldn't otherwise be doing, make
> them as radical as you think you can realistically achieve, and go for it. This
> idea has a lot of appeal. It is an intuitive sense of your own significance in the
> scheme of things, and if you're coming in as an outsider, as most political ap-
> pointees are, to your organization, that you would bring to it something, which
> rationalized, in effect, your characteristics as an outsider.[1]

Danzig notes that this view of leadership in a public organization has roots in
the private sector models drawn from the business community and from what he
views as the biblical concept of leadership. "It is a Moses-like notion. Preach a
new vision. Go up on the mountain and see it. Then lead the chosen people, if
necessary, through 40 years in the wilderness to the Promised Land." For Danzig,
however, this approach to leadership is wrong, misleading, and—in many situations—dangerous. "You have only to look at how many visions are, in fact, fundamentally wrong to appreciate how potentially misguided this notion of operation is."[2]

What, then, is an alternative approach to leadership that allows a public sector
leader to think about ways to approach accountability? How should Raymond
Wilson think about his job?

Richard Danzig challenges a new appointee to listen to what the organization
is saying about what it cares about and what it values. "Many of these propositions have the ring of gospel and an elegant and uplifting character but, in fact, in
many respects some of the most interesting and important things that the organization says about itself it says in the form of its cliches." Danzig found that the
propositions he found within the Department of the Navy were not translated
into the day-to-day life of the organization.

> The most crucial question for the organization after you listen to it is to look
> hard at these propositions and see what they mean in practice. When we began
> to mind that, we started to come up with all kinds of propositions that could
> fairly be described as radical. Indeed, in the end, in many dimensions revolu-
> tionary, but this had the enormous advantage that these were all derived from
> premises that everyone accepted and that were in no way personal to me or to
> the idiosyncrasies of my vision, and in themselves got beyond controversy.[3]

It is a real challenge for a new secretary of HHS to find a way to identify what
that department cares about and what it values. It is this combination of values

and premises that sets the backdrop for any effort to respond to the constantly changing and conflicting set of accountability expectations that have been discussed in this book.

What are the premises embedded within the cultures of the Department of Health and Human Services that Raymond Wilson can describe and classify? There are at least five such premises that become a new secretary's point of departure: (1) the life and death nature of many HHS issues; (2) the acknowledgment that a significant number of programs and policies live with controversy and conflicting values; (3) the recognition that most of the HHS programs call on the federal government to be partners, not controllers, in achieving the goals of programs; (4) the importance and reality of a range of well-honed professional identities within the department; and (5) the fragmentation of approaches that stems from the diversity of programs and client groups found within HHS.

A MATTER OF LIFE AND DEATH

Many of the programs found within the department's portfolio involve issues that directly affect the life chances of many Americans. Programs that deal with health and illness are obvious examples of this reality. Whether focused on research dealing with the treatment of HIV/AIDS, trying to find the causes of breast cancer, or mapping the genome to create protocols to deal with differences between individuals, HHS programs are understood to lead to real consequences for the nation's citizens. Similarly, efforts to regulate food and drugs are put in place to ensure that the products purchased by consumers are safe and actually achieve the results that are promised. Still other HHS health programs actually provide services to those who do not have alternative forms of treatment available to them (such as health services to Native Americans, rural citizens, and individuals who cannot afford or do not have access to other health services).

But beyond the health programs, other HHS efforts actually provide life chances and protect those who otherwise would be left without other sources of support. Financial assistance to those without other support is made available through the welfare block grant. Funds are made available through the Low Income Heating and Energy Assistance Program (LIHEAP) program to those who have high energy bills and inadequate income to pay them. Resources are provided to help parents pay for adequate child care and to provide food for the elderly who do not have the physical or financial means to arrange meals for themselves.

Whether or not the federal government intervenes directly in providing these services (or, instead, provides financial support to others who actually provide the service), one of the important values in the department is to acknowledge the role that it plays in assisting others.

CONTROVERSY AND
CONFLICTING VALUES

Some federal departments operate with relatively clear support from the general public in regard to the goals of their programs and policies. Perhaps few departments match the Department of Transportation's general support within the society; highways and transportation safety are clearly "motherhood and apple pie" values within the society. Other departments have some level of controversy attached to their programs; for example, the Environmental Protection Agency, the Department of the Interior, and the Department of Agriculture have to balance the value of environmental protection with that of economic development.

It is almost impossible to find a program area within HHS that does not have to deal with controversy and conflicting values within the society. In many areas, there is strong conflict within the citizenry about the appropriate role of the federal government or, indeed, whether any government should be involved at all. Over the years there has been a constant movement back and forth between responsibilities assumed by the federal government and responsibilities and funds devolved to state or local governments or other entities. For example, should the federal government attempt to establish standards as a bottom line in programs such as day care or for medical care for the needy? Should the federal government be responsible for ensuring that individuals without other sources of support receive cash assistance? Is it appropriate for the federal government to regulate industries such as pharmaceuticals or, conversely, to find ways to encourage that private sector to develop products that meet social needs? Should the federal government support programs that serve as a basic safety net in areas such as health insurance for children when the private sector does not provide that service?

In other areas, some HHS programs represent strategies that conflict with other program areas. These conflicts sometimes occur because the society has not reached agreement about the most effective or most appropriate mode of intervention. Sometimes funds are used for research to develop new treatment procedures that will not be reimbursed by other federal health programs. Similarly, attempts to develop drug prevention efforts at times collide with other efforts (such as needle exchange) to protect the health of drug users.

Prohibitions against the use of human embryos in research protocols may inhibit the research that would lead to new understanding of treatment potentials in other areas. In still other cases, the federal government supports programs that seek to improve the training and quality of those who provide services, setting quality standards that may result in the need to ration or limit the provision of services. Yet, at the same time, other programs are designed to increase access to and thus demand for services without focusing on the availability of providers.

THE FEDERAL GOVERNMENT AS PARTNER

Unlike the social programs of many other countries, numerous programs found within the Department of Health and Human Services have depended on others to ensure that services are provided to the nation's citizens. During the New Deal, expanding social programs greatly increased the federal role in those efforts. In many of these programs, such as the programs of the Indian Health Services and the Public Health Service, federal staff actually provided the services. Other programs, however, such as several of those created as a result of the 1935 Social Security Act and its amendments, provided federal dollars but called on states and localities to deliver the services (and, in some instances, also contribute funds to match the federal dollars). Still, the federal government often assumed that its role was preeminent and that the other actors who were involved should defer to the federal controls.

By the end of the twentieth century, however, the changes that took place in the design of programs such as Temporary Assistance to Needy Families (TANF) and the Maternal and Child Health programs (moving them into block grant constructs) diminished the levers that federal agencies could use to evoke change. Devolution of authority away from Washington meant that it was more difficult to defend the tenet that Washington always knows best. As the structural changes occurred, some federal officials were becoming more aware that the federal government was becoming much less of a controller than it was a facilitator in program implementation. Also, in many instances, federal agencies were unable to pull the political and fiscal strings that were required to change state or local practices. Despite the rhetoric of control, federal agency behavior was more likely to call on bluffing strategies than on sanctions that might have been legally available.

By the beginning of the Clinton administration, the concept of partnerships was used to describe the emergent federal role. HHS no longer defined its position as that of a controller but pointed to changes in the way that programs looked at their relationships with state and local government. The language of the reinvention movement was used to give state and local governments more control over programs and their own ability to produce results. The idea of partnership—acknowledging that the federal government shares responsibility for the achievement of program goals—replaced earlier descriptions of the federal role. Partners were defined to include not only state and local governments but also Native American tribes and a wide range of nongovernmental actors, particularly groups from the not-for-profit sector. Opening the door to the array of groups with whom the program units in the department do business created a real challenge. The department was called on to devise approaches that would allow it to carry out its policy responsibilities and to operate within the existing framework of program structure and design. Yet, concurrently, HHS had to work effectively with those outside the department to carry out these responsibilities. The need for bipartisanship naturally flowed from this set of changes, since the partners involved in programs were likely to be drawn from all sides of the political spectrum.

Although the partnership concept became a part of the rhetoric within HHS, it was not always easy to put it into operation. The partnership approach required federal officials to acknowledge that their role was much more variegated than it had been in the past. In most instances, relying on the traditional process of issuing regulations and guidelines was no longer possible. Federal officials were challenged to learn how to be facilitators, brokers, and often behind-the-scenes actors in the implementation process. New policy instruments were emphasized that made more sense in the altered environment (such as support of peer-to-peer technical assistance efforts, allowing grantees to find ways to learn from one another).

A RANGE OF WELL-HONED PROFESSIONAL IDENTITIES

In some respects, one could describe the staff of HHS as a variation on Noah's ark: there seem to be two of most living staff species found within its organizational borders. Although most contemporary public organizations do contain personnel drawn from many fields of expertise, HHS is compounded in complexity because many of the staff have expert knowledge in well-defined professional areas. The federal personnel system is sometimes defended as a generic arrangement in which career public servants are subject to legal and administrative controls. But many of the implementation tasks in HHS call for individuals who are trained and evaluated by a set of standards defined by other members of a particular profession.[4]

The range of professions found in HHS varies in regard to the status of the group within the society, the ability of the government agency to compete with the private sector for staff, and the relationship between those in the public sector and those outside. The individuals who work in the NIH, for example, include the nation's top researchers in specific fields of study, many of whom continue to work as bench scientists and have been responsible for major scientific discoveries. High-status professionals are also found in the CDC and the FDA, both of which employ individuals with expert training in their fields. CDC involvement in identifying and treating health epidemics across the globe has made staff experience the basis for Hollywood films. The research into and investigation of problems that have been undertaken by FDA staff members are responsible for tracking down unsafe products and making them unavailable for purchase.

There are other professions found within HHS that are less visible. The NIH includes staff members who specialize in the management of research and development programs. Although they are less visible to the general public, they are known within a narrower field of specialization. Staff attorneys within the department often develop a field of specialization in the law and are active in their professional organizations. It is difficult for HHS to attract state-of-the-art computer staff because of competition from the private sector, but it does have many individuals with computer training who have attempted to keep up with developments in the field. Other department staff are trained in child development, social work, gerontology, research and evaluation, public health, and other related professional fields and value their identity within those fields of practice.

These externally defined relationships provide a point of departure for many HHS staff members. They give career staffers the ability to stay up-to-date with developments in their fields. They establish standards and quality measures that define objectives for staffers. But these external relationships also make it more difficult for agency leaders to treat their staff in traditional bureaucratic ways, relying on legal and administrative controls to elicit behavior.

FRAGMENTATION OF APPROACHES

It is difficult to view the whole of HHS as a unified entity. Rather, it seems much more accurate to characterize it as a fragmented organization. And some of the units within the organization have long been de facto independent agencies with strong identities and unique cultures. The fragmentation present in the department stems from the cumulative effects of shared powers between various institutions of government, the large number of programs within HHS, the conflicts between approaches, and the multiple groups that are affected by its programs. Although there are subsystems (or, more likely, subsubsystems) within HHS that can be described as policy communities, even those entities often contain aspects of fragmentation. Members of such communities are not always able to describe others with interest in a particular policy field or find ways to develop relationships with them that reflect common features or shared orientations and ways of thinking.[5]

Fragmentation has many consequences. Policy fragmentation emerges when, as Kingdon noted, the right hand does not know what the left hand is doing.[6] In addition, fragmentation generates policy instability—that is, situations in which policy design moves and shifts when various aspects of the policy community are predominant over others.

No matter where one looks, it becomes clear that the American fragmented structure of government actually prohibits any institution or actor from viewing the department as a whole. Despite the illusion that the president's budget is a single entity, in reality that budget is developed through a process in which specific parts of the HHS budget emerge from different parts of the OMB. The scale and scope of HHS programs make it almost impossible for any single individual to focus on detailed crosscuts or interrelationships between elements.

Similarly, the fragmented nature of congressional authority also reinforces the tendency for members to look at specific programs individually, disaggregating the maze of programs and policies into small bits that make the system more comprehensible.

The multiple nodes of this variegated system provide a range of entry points for groups and individuals who seek to influence the development of policy. The system creates a set of possibilities that resemble the contemporary department store—an array of individual boutiques organized not by the product for sale but by the producer of that product.

LIVING IN A WEB OF ACCOUNTABILITY EXPECTATIONS

I have tried to convey a sense of the fluidity and turbulence that make the task of managing the Department of Health and Human Services challenging, at the least. The secretary of the department has been described as an accountable juggler—someone who has to balance multiple actors and pressures. Dropping one of those elements not only has political consequences but it also has substantive consequences for those individuals who are affected by the HHS programs as well as for the thousands of career public servants and others who make those programs come alive.

One could view the world that the HHS secretary inhabits as a random world, where processes are random and results emerge strictly out of luck. But as John Kingdon argued, the fluidity of the policy process does not mean that structure is absent from the process.[7] The attributes of the agenda-setting process that he describes are also found in the world of a cabinet secretary attempting to manage policy, politics, and processes. His model is both structured and flexible enough to contain what he calls "residual randomness." He calls on theories of complexity and chaos theory as well as on the garbage can model to promote an understanding of a system with several properties: pattern and structure in complicated, fluid, and seemingly unpredictable phenomena; residual randomness; and historically contingent behavior.[8]

The ability to respond to these attributes calls for leaders who are highly skilled, able to listen to the cacophony of voices around them, and capable of adapting to constantly changing circumstances. The task of leading the Department of Health and Human Services is incredibly challenging. But there are few other public organizations that allow an individual to make such a difference in the lives of American citizens.

Notes

1. Richard Danzig, Secretary of the Navy, Webb Lecture, presented at the National Academy of Public Administration, Washington, D.C., November 17, 2000.

2. Ibid.

3. Ibid.

4. See discussion in James Q. Wilson, *Bureaucracy: What Government Agencies Do and Why They Do It* (New York: Basic Books, 1989), 149.

5. See discussion of policy communities in John W. Kingdon, *Agendas, Alternatives, and Public Policies,* 2d ed. (New York: HarperCollins, 1995), 117–119.

6. Ibid., 119.

7. Ibid., 222.

8. Ibid., 224.

Appendix 1.
HHS Historical Highlights

The roots of the U.S. Department of Health and Human Services go back to the earliest days of the nation.

1798   The first Marine Hospital, a forerunner of today's Public Health Service, was established to care for seafarers.

1862   President Abraham Lincoln appointed a chemist, Charles M. Wetherill, to serve in the new Department of Agriculture. This was the beginning of the Bureau of Chemistry, forerunner to the Food and Drug Administration.

1887   The federal government opened a one-room laboratory on Staten Island for research on disease, thereby planting the seed that was to grow into the National Institutes of Health.

1906   Congress passed the first Food and Drug Act, authorizing the government to monitor the purity of foods and the safety of medicines, now a responsibility of the Food and Drug Administration.

1912   President Theodore Roosevelt's first White House Conference urged creation of a Children's Bureau to combat exploitation of children.

1935   Congress passed the Social Security Act.

1939   Related federal activities in the fields of health, education, social insurance, and human services were brought together under the new Federal Security Agency.

1946   The Communicable Disease Center was established, forerunner of the Centers for Disease Control and Prevention.

1953   The cabinet-level Department of Health, Education and Welfare, was created under President Dwight D. Eisenhower.

1955   The Salk polio vaccine was licensed.

1961   The first White House Conference on Aging was held.

1962   The Migrant Health Act, providing support for clinics serving agricultural workers, was passed.

1964   The surgeon general released the first *Surgeon General's Report on Smoking and Health*.

1965   The Medicare and Medicaid programs were created, making comprehensive health care available to millions of Americans. The Older Americans Act created the nutritional and social programs run by the Administration on Aging, and the Head Start program was created.

1966   The International Smallpox Eradication program was established. The Community Health Center and Migrant Health Center programs were launched.

1970   The National Health Service Corps was created.

1971   The National Cancer Act was signed into law.

1975   The Child Support Enforcement program was established.

1977   The Health Care Financing Administration was created to manage Medicare and Medicaid separately from the Social Security Administration. Led by the U.S. Public Health Service, smallpox was eradicated worldwide.

1979   The Department of Education Organization Act was signed into law, providing for a separate Department of Education.

1980   HEW became the Department of Health and Human Services. Federal funding was provided to states for foster care and adoption assistance.

1981   The Acquired Immune Deficiency Syndrome, AIDS, was identified.

1984   The National Organ Transplantation Act was signed into law.

1988   The JOBS program was created, and federal support for child care was initiated.

The McKinney Act was signed into law, providing health care to the homeless.

1989   The Agency for Health Care Policy and Research was created.

1990   The Human Genome Project was established. The Nutrition Labeling and Education Act was signed into law. The Ryan White Comprehensive AIDS Resource Emergency (CARE) Act began in 1990 to provide support for communities to help people with AIDS.

1993   The Vaccines for Children Program was established, providing free immunizations to all children in low-income families.

1994   NIH-supported scientists discovered the genes responsible for many cases of hereditary colon cancer, inherited breast cancer, and the most common type of kidney cancer.

1995   The Social Security Administration became an independent agency on March 31.

1996   Welfare reform was enacted under the Personal Responsibility and Work Opportunity Reconciliation Act. Regulations were published providing for FDA regulation of tobacco products to prevent use of tobacco by minors.

1997   The State Children's Health Insurance Program was established.

1998   The Initiative to Eliminate Racial and Ethnic Disparities in Health was launched. The initiative focuses on six key areas of health: infant mortality, cancer screening and management, cardiovascular disease, diabetes, HIV/AIDS, and immunizations.

1999   The Ticket to Work and Work Incentives Improvement Act of 1999 was signed, making it possible for millions of Americans with disabilities to join the workforce without fear of losing their Medicaid and Medicare coverage. It also modernized the employment services system for people with disabilities.

2000   AIDS was dropped from the top fifteen causes of death. Scientists completed the map of the human genome.

2001   The Health Care Financing Administration was renamed the Center for Medicare and Medicaid Services.

Appendix 2.
Secretaries of HEW and HHS

1.	Oveta Culp Hobby	April 11, 1953–July 31, 1955
2.	Marion B. Folsom	August 1, 1955–July 31, 1958
3.	Arthur S. Flemming	August 1, 1958–January 19, 1961
4.	Abraham Ribicoff	January 21, 1961–July 13, 1962
5.	Anthony J. Celebrezze	July 31, 1962–August 17, 1965
6.	John W. Gardner	August 18, 1965–March 1, 1968
7.	Wilbur J. Cohen	May 16, 1968–January 20, 1969
8.	Robert H. Finch	January 21, 1969–June 23, 1970
9.	Elliot L. Richardson	June 24, 1970–January 29, 1973
10.	Caspar W. Weinberger	February 12, 1973–August 8, 1975
11.	David Mathews	August 8, 1975–January 20, 1977
12.	Joseph A. Califano Jr.	January 25, 1977–August 3, 1979
13.	Patricia Roberts Harris	August 3, 1979–January 20, 1981
14.	Richard S. Schweiker	January 22, 1981–February 3, 1983
15.	Margaret M. Heckler	March 9, 1983–December 13, 1985
16.	Otis R. Bowen, M.D.	December 13, 1985–January 20, 1989
17.	Louis W. Sullivan, M.D.	March 1, 1989–January 20, 1993
18.	Donna E. Shalala	January 22, 1993–January 20, 2001
19.	Tommy G. Thompson	February 2, 2001–

Appendix 3.
HHS Regional Offices

Region I
Boston, Mass.
Areas: Conn., Maine, Mass., N.H., R.I., Vt.

Region II
New York, N.Y.
Areas: N.J., N.Y., Puerto Rico, Virgin Islands

Region III
Philadelphia, Pa.
Areas: Del., D.C., Md., Pa., Va., W.Va.

Region IV
Atlanta, Ga.
Areas: Ala., Fla., Ga., Ky., Miss., N.C., S.C., Tenn.

Region V
Chicago, Ill.
Areas: Ill., Ind., Mich., Minn., Ohio, Wisc.

Region VI
Dallas, Tex.
Areas: Ark., La., N.Mex., Okla., Tex.

Region VII
Kansas City, Mo.
Areas: Iowa, Kans., Mo., Nebr.

Region VIII
Denver, Colo.
Areas: Colo., Mont., N.Dak., S.Dak., Utah, Wyo.

Region IX
San Francisco, Calif.
Areas: Ariz., Calif., Hawaii, Nev., Guam, Pacific Islands, American Samoa

Region X
Seattle, Wash.
Areas: Alaska, Idaho, Ore., Wash.

Appendix 4.
The HHS Portfolio

The Administration for Children and Families (ACF)

The Administration for Children and Families is responsible for federal programs that promote the economic and social well-being of families, children, individuals, and communities. ACF programs aim to achieve the following: families and individuals empowered to increase their own economic independence and productivity; strong, healthy, supportive communities that have a positive impact on the quality of life and the development of children; partnerships with individuals, front-line service providers, communities, American Indian tribes, Native Alaskan communities, states, and Congress that enable solutions that transcend traditional agency boundaries; services planned, reformed, and integrated to improve needed access; and a strong commitment to working with people with developmental disabilities, refugees, and migrants to address their needs, strengths, and abilities. Several programs within ACF are of special interest.

Temporary Assistance for Needy Families (TANF) On August 22, 1996, President Clinton signed into law the Personal Responsibility and Work Opportunity Reconciliation Act of 1996, a comprehensive bipartisan welfare reform plan that dramatically changed the nation's welfare system into one that requires work in exchange for time-limited assistance. The TANF program replaced the former AFDC and JOBS programs. In TANF, states and territories operate programs; under the new law, tribes have the option to run their own TANF programs. States, territories, and tribes each receive a block grant allocation; states have a maintenance of effort requirement. The total federal block grant is $16.5 billion each year through fiscal year 2002. The block grant covers benefits, administrative expenses, and services. States, territories, and tribes determine eligibility and benefit levels and services provided to needy families, and there is no longer a federal entitlement.

Head Start Head Start and Early Head Start are comprehensive child development programs that serve children from birth to age five, pregnant women, and their families. They are child-focused programs and have the overall goal of increasing the school readiness of young children in low-income families. The Head Start program is administered by the Head Start Bureau, the Administration on Children, Youth and Families (ACYF), and Administration for Children and Families (ACF). Grants are awarded by the ACF regional offices and the Head Start Bureau's American Indian and Migrant Program branches directly to local public agencies, private organizations, Indian tribes, and school systems for the purpose of operating Head Start programs at the community level.

The Head Start program has a long tradition of delivering comprehensive and high-quality services designed to foster healthy development in low-income children. Head Start grantee and delegate agencies provide a range of individualized services in the areas of education and early childhood development; medical, dental, and mental health; nutrition; and parent involvement. In addition, the entire range of Head Start

142

services is responsive and appropriate to the developmental, ethnic, cultural, and linguistic heritage and experience of each child and family.

Foster Care/Adoption Assistance/Independent Living For those children who cannot remain safely in their homes, foster care provides a stable environment that ensures a child's safety and well-being while his or her parents attempt to resolve the problems that led to the out-of-home placement, or when the family cannot be reunified, until the child can be placed permanently with an adoptive family. Foster Care and Adoption Assistance programs provide federal matching funds to states, which directly administer the programs. Children in foster care numbered more than 560,000 in September 1998, up from 340,000 in 1988. Most of these children will return to their homes, but more than 120,000 cannot return safely. Many of these children are considered to have "special needs" because they are older; members of minority or sibling groups; or physically, mentally, or emotionally disabled. They often need special assistance in finding adoptive homes. Currently, more than 100,000 children receive Title IV-E adoption assistance, which is a subsidy to families.

Child Abuse and Neglect Programs Just over 900,000 children were victims of substantiated child abuse and neglect in 1998, and the states reported 1,100 child fatalities from maltreatment. About half were cases of neglect; a quarter, physical abuse; and about one in seven, sexual abuse. Maltreated children were found in all income, racial, and ethnic groups, and incidence rates were similar in urban, suburban, and rural communities. The Child Abuse and Neglect Program funds states and grantees in several different programs authorized by the Child Abuse and Neglect Prevention and Treatment Act (CAPTA). The programs provide funds and technical assistance for prevention and intervention; support research, service improvement programs, and demonstration projects; collect data about the problem, its consequences, and the effectiveness of prevention and treatment services; facilitate information dissemination and exchange; and support policy development and professional education.

The Administration on Aging (AoA)

In response to the growing number of older people and their diverse needs, the Older Americans Act of 1965 as amended calls for a range of programs that offer services and opportunities for older Americans, especially those at risk of losing their independence. AoA is the federal focal point and advocate agency for older persons and their concerns. In this role, AoA works to heighten awareness among other federal agencies, organizations, groups, and the public about the valuable contributions that older Americans make to the nation and alerts them to the needs of vulnerable older people. Through information and referral and outreach efforts at the community level, AoA seeks to educate older people and their caregivers about the benefits and services available to help them.

AoA works closely with its nationwide network of regional offices and state and area agencies on aging to plan, coordinate, and develop community-level systems of services that meet the unique needs of individual older persons and their caregivers. The Administration on Aging collaborates with federal agencies, national organizations, and representatives of business to ensure that, whenever possible, their programs and resources are targeted to the elderly and coordinated with those of the network on aging.

AoA administers key programs at the federal level mandated under various titles of the Older Americans Act. These programs help vulnerable older persons remain in their own homes by providing supportive services. Other programs offer opportunities for older Americans to enhance their health and to be active contributors to their families, communities, and the nation through employment and volunteer programs.

Program funding is allocated to each state agency on aging, based on the number of older persons in the state, to plan, develop, and coordinate systems of supportive in-home and community-based services. Most states are divided into planning and service areas (PSAs) so that programs can be effectively developed and targeted to meet the unique needs of the elderly residing in that area. Nationwide some 660 area agencies on aging (AAAs) receive funds from their respective state agencies on aging to plan, develop, coordinate, and arrange for services in each PSA. In rural areas an AAA may serve the needs of elderly people living in many different counties, whereas other AAAs may serve the elderly living in a single city.

The Agency for Healthcare Research and Quality (AHRQ)

On December 6, 1999, President Clinton signed the Healthcare Research and Quality Act of 1999, reauthorizing the Agency for Health Care Policy and Research (AHCPR) until the end of fiscal year 2005. In 1999 AHCPR was renamed the Agency for Healthcare Research and Quality (AHRQ). The new name is significant because it reaffirms that AHRQ is a scientific research agency; corrects the misperception that the agency determines federal health care policies and regulations by removing "policy" from the agency name, and adds the word quality to the name, thus establishing AHRQ as the leading federal agency on quality-of-care research, with new responsibility to coordinate all federal quality improvement efforts and health services research. The agency has been fulfilling this function since 1998 through its leadership role in the federal Quality Interagency Coordination (QuIC) Task Force.

AHRQ is the lead agency charged with supporting research designed to improve the quality of health care, reduce its cost, improve patient safety, decrease medical errors, and broaden access to essential services. AHRQ sponsors and conducts research that provides evidence-based information on health care outcomes; quality; and cost, use, and access. The information helps health care decision makers—patients and clinicians, health system leaders, and policy makers—make more informed decisions and improve the quality of health care services. The legislation also positions the agency as a "science partner," working collaboratively with the public and private sectors to improve the quality and safety of patient care.

The Agency for Toxic Substances and Disease Registry (ATSDR)

In 1980 Congress created the Agency for Toxic Substances and Disease Registry to implement the health-related sections of laws that protect the public from hazardous wastes and environmental spills of hazardous substances. The Comprehensive Environmental Response, Compensation, and Liability Act of 1980 (CERCLA), commonly known as the "Superfund" Act, provided the congressional mandate to remove or clean up abandoned and inactive hazardous waste sites and to provide federal assistance in toxic emergencies. As the lead agency within the Public Health Service for implementing the health-related provisions of CERCLA, ATSDR is charged under the Superfund Act to assess the presence and nature of health hazards at specific Superfund sites, to help prevent or reduce further exposure and the illnesses that result from such exposures, and to expand the knowledge base about health effects from exposure to hazardous substances.

The mission of ATSDR is to prevent exposure and adverse human health effects and diminished quality of life associated with exposure to hazardous substances from waste sites, unplanned releases, and other sources of pollution present in the environment.

The Centers for Disease Control and Prevention (CDC)

The Centers for Disease Control and Prevention, created in 1946, serves as the national focus for developing and applying disease prevention and control, environmental health, and health promotion and educational activities designed to improve the health of the people of the United States. The CDC is recognized as the leading federal agency for protecting the health and safety of people at home and abroad, providing credible information to enhance health decisions, and promoting health through strong partnerships.

The CDC emphasizes health prevention. By charting decisive courses of action, collecting the right information, and working closely with other health and community organizations, the CDC has been putting science into action to tackle important health problems since 1946. With more than 8,500 employees across the country, the CDC plays a critical role in protecting the public from the most widespread, deadly, and mysterious threats against our health today and tomorrow.

The CDC seeks to accomplish its mission by working with partners throughout the nation and world to monitor health, detect and investigate health problems, conduct research to enhance prevention, develop and advocate sound public health policies, implement prevention strategies, promote healthy behaviors, foster safe and healthful environments, and provide leadership and training.

The CDC has developed and sustained many vital partnerships with public and private entities that improve service to the American people. In fiscal year 2000, the workforce of the CDC comprised approximately 8,500 staff in 170 disciplines with a public health focus. Although the CDC's national headquarters are in Atlanta, Georgia, more than 2,000 CDC employees work at other locations, including forty-seven state health departments. Approximately 120 are assigned overseas in forty-five countries. The CDC includes eleven centers, institutes, and offices. In fiscal year 2000, the CDC's total funding level was approximately $4 billion. This comprised funding the CDC received from all sources, including its annual appropriation, reimbursable income, and emergency funding in fiscal year 2000.

Infectious diseases, such as HIV/AIDS and tuberculosis, have the ability to destroy lives, strain community resources, and even threaten nations. In today's global environment, new diseases have the potential to spread across the world in a matter of days, or even hours, making early detection and action more important than ever. The CDC plays a critical role in controlling these diseases, traveling at a moment's notice to investigate outbreaks abroad or at home.

By assisting state and local health departments, the CDC works to protect the public every day: from using innovative "fingerprinting" technology to identifying a foodborne illness, to evaluating a family violence prevention program in an urban community; from training partners in HIV education to protecting children from vaccine preventable diseases through immunizations.

The Food and Drug Administration (FDA)

Congress laid the foundation for modern food and drug law when it passed the Food and Drugs Act of 1906. This first nationwide consumer protection law made it illegal to distribute misbranded or adulterated foods, drinks, and drugs across state lines. Every day, every American comes in contact with a host of products regulated by the Food and Drug Administration, from the most common food ingredients to complex medical and surgical devices, lifesaving drugs, and radiation-emitting consumer and medical products. In fact, FDA-regulated products account for about twenty-five cents of every consumer dollar spent in the United States.

Stated most simply, the FDA's mission is to promote and protect the public health by helping safe and effective products reach the market in a timely way and by monitoring products for continued safety after they are in use. The FDA has streamlined its review process in recent years to help speed important new medical treatments to patients. For example, the average review time for an innovative new drug is now only six months, and some drugs and other products have been approved even faster. Products receiving accelerated reviews include new treatments for breast cancer; a rapid, reliable diagnostic test for pneumonia; and devices to improve the monitoring and treatment of diabetes.

The last several years have seen an increase in the number and severity of foodborne illnesses around the country. The FDA has launched a major initiative to prevent the spread of these food-related infections. The initiative promotes safer food-handling practices by producers and consumers and more effective detection, tracking, and prevention of food-borne illness. A similar initiative aims at improving the safety practices in the blood-banking and plasma industries. The FDA works continuously to improve donor screening, blood testing, and other quality control procedures in blood donation and blood banking. The agency helps the industry develop and use new, more accurate tests to detect hazards in the nation's blood supply.

The FDA's regulatory approaches are as varied as the products it regulates. Some products—such as new drugs and complex medical devices—must be proven safe and effective before companies can put them on the market. Other products—such as x-ray machines and microwave ovens—must measure up to performance standards. And some products—such as cosmetics and dietary supplements—can be marketed with no prior approval. At the heart of all the FDA's product evaluation decisions is a judgment about whether a new product's benefits to users will outweigh its risks. No regulated product is totally risk-free, so these judgments are important. The FDA will allow a product to present more of a risk when its potential benefit is great—especially for products used to treat serious, life-threatening conditions.

Medical products need to be proven safe and effective before they can be used by patients. The product categories covered by this requirement include medicines used for the treatment and prevention of disease; biologics—a product category that includes vaccines, blood products, biotechnology products, and gene therapy; and medical devices. Although the FDA regulates all medical devices, from very simple items like tongue depressors or thermometers to very complex technologies such as heart pacemakers and dialysis machines, only the most complex medical devices are reviewed by the agency before marketing.

The Centers for Medicare and Medicaid Services (CMS)

The Centers for Medicare and Medicaid Services, known as the Health Care Financing Administration before 2001, runs the Medicare and Medicaid programs. These two national health care programs benefit about 75 million Americans. And with the Health Resources and Services Administration, the CMS runs the Children's Health Insurance Program, a program that is expected to cover many of the approximately 10 million uninsured children in the United States. The CMS also regulates all laboratory testing (except research) performed on humans in the United States. Approximately 158,000 laboratory entities fall within its regulatory responsibility. With the Departments of Labor and the Treasury, the CMS helps millions of Americans and small companies get and keep health insurance coverage and helps eliminate discrimination based on health status for people buying health insurance.

The CMS spends more than $360 billion a year buying health care services for beneficiaries of Medicare, Medicaid, and the Children's Health Insurance Program. The CMS ensures that these programs are properly run by their contractors and state agencies; establishes policies for paying health care providers; conducts research on the effectiveness of various methods of health care management, treatment, and financing; and assesses the quality of health care facilities and services.

The agency has a comprehensive program to combat fraud and abuse. Working with other federal departments and state and local governments, it takes strong enforcement action against those who commit fraud and abuse, protects taxpayer dollars, and guarantees security for the Medicare, Medicaid, and Child Health Insurance programs.

Agency staff members working in the Baltimore, Maryland, headquarters and in ten regional offices nationwide oversee the CMS programs. The headquarters staff is responsible for national program direction. The regional office staff provides the agency with the local presence necessary for quality customer service and oversight.

The agency's vision is to lead the nation's health care system toward improved health for all. Its goals are to

• Protect and improve beneficiary health and satisfaction
• Promote the fiscal integrity of programs
• Purchase the best value health care for beneficiaries
• Promote beneficiary and public understanding of the agency and its programs
• Foster excellence in the design and administration of programs
• Provide leadership in the broader public interest to improve health

The Health Resources and Services Administration (HRSA)

The Health Resources and Services Administration directs national health programs that improve the nation's health by ensuring equitable access to comprehensive, quality health care for all. HRSA works to improve and extend life for people living with HIV/AIDS, to provide primary health care to medically underserved people, to serve women and children through state programs, and to train a health workforce that is both diverse and motivated to work in underserved communities.

HRSA is the leading federal agency in promoting access to health care services that create and improve the nation's health. With a statutory emphasis on special needs, underserved, and vulnerable populations, HRSA mobilizes its bureaus, programs, staff, and partners to ensure access to quality health care. HRSA is an agency with multiple programs but with a single strategic goal: to ensure 100 percent access to health care and 0 percent disparities for all Americans. It works to establish alliances and partnerships with a broad array of organizations, ranging from state and local governments to foundations and corporations. In order to support its goal, HRSA has established four strategies: (1) eliminate barriers to care, (2) eliminate health disparities, (3) ensure quality of care, and (4) improve public health and health care systems. Its portfolio includes a range of programs or initiatives designed to increase access to care, improve quality, and safeguard the health and well-being of the nation's most vulnerable.

HRSA accomplishes its mission by working with states and communities that form the foundation for developing integrated service systems and the appropriate health workforce to help ensure access to essential high-quality health care. It ensures that these systems take into account cultural and linguistic factors, geographic location, and economic circumstances, and it assists states and communities to identify and address unmet service needs and workforce gaps in the health care system. It also promotes continuous quality improvement in the delivery of health services and the education of health professionals; supports innovative partnerships to promote effective, integrated systems of care for all population groups; and promotes the recruitment, training, and retention of a culturally and linguistically competent and diverse health care workforce.

The Indian Health Service (IHS)

The Indian Health Service, an agency of the U.S. Public Health Service, is responsible for providing federal health services to American Indians and Alaska Natives. The provision of health services to members of federally recognized tribes grew out of the special government-to-government relationship between the federal government and Indian tribes. This relationship, established in 1787, is based on Article I, Section 8, of the Constitution and has been given form and substance by numerous treaties, laws, Supreme Court decisions, and executive orders. As the principal federal health care provider and health advocate for Indian people, the IHS strives for maximum tribal involvement in meeting its goal of raising their health status to the highest possible level. With an annual appropriation of approximately $2.2 billion, the IHS currently provides health services to approximately 1.5 million of the nation's 2 million American Indians and Alaska Natives who belong to more than 557 federally recognized tribes in thirty-four states.

The IHS combines preventive measures (involving environmental, educational, and outreach activities) and therapeutic measures into a single national health system. Within these broad categories, the agency carries out special initiatives in such areas as injury control, alcoholism, diabetes, and mental health. The IHS appropriates most of its funds for American Indians who live on or near reservations. Congress also has authorized programs that provide some access to care for American Indians and Alaska Natives who live in urban areas.

IHS services are provided directly and also through tribally contracted and operated health programs. Health services also include health care purchased from more than two thousand private providers. As of March 1996, the federal system consisted of 37 hospitals, 64 health centers, 50 health stations, and 5 school health centers. In addition, 34 urban Indian health projects provide a variety of health and referral services. The IHS clinical staff consists of approximately 840 physicians, 380 dentists, 100 physician assistants, and 2,580 nurses. The IHS also employs allied health professionals, such as nutritionists, health administrators, engineers, and medical records administrators.

The National Institutes of Health (NIH)

Begun as a one-room Laboratory of Hygiene in 1887, the National Institutes of Health today is one of the world's foremost medical research centers, and the federal focal point for medical research in the United States. The NIH mission is to uncover new knowledge that will lead to better health for everyone. The NIH works toward that mission by conducting research in its own laboratories; supporting the research of nonfederal scientists in universities, medical schools, hospitals, and research institutions throughout the country and abroad; helping in the training of research investigators; and fostering communication of medical information.

Comprised of twenty-five separate institutes and centers, the NIH has seventy-five buildings on more than 300 acres in Bethesda, Maryland. From a total budget of about $300 in 1887, the NIH budget has grown to more than $17.8 billion in 2000. Simply described, the goal of NIH research is to acquire new knowledge to help prevent, detect, diagnose, and treat disease and disability, from the rarest genetic disorder to the common cold. A principal concern of the NIH is to invest wisely the tax dollars entrusted to it for the support and conduct of biomedical research.

Approximately 82 percent of the investment is made through grants and contracts supporting research and training in more than 2,000 research institutions throughout the United States and abroad. In fact, NIH grantees are located in every state in the country. These grants and contracts comprise the NIH Extramural Research Program. Approximately 10 percent of the budget goes to the NIH's Intramural Research Programs, the more than 2,000 projects conducted mainly in its own laboratories. About 8 percent of the budget is for both intramural and extramural research support costs.

Final decisions about funding extramural research are made at the NIH headquarters. But long before this happens, the process begins with an idea that an individual scientist describes in a written application for a research grant. The project might be small, or it might involve millions of dollars. The project might become useful immediately as a diagnostic test or new treatment, or it might involve studies of basic biological processes whose practical value may not be apparent for many years.

Each research grant application undergoes a peer review process. A panel of scientific experts, primarily from outside the government, who are active and productive researchers in the biomedical sciences, first evaluates the scientific merit of the application. Then, a national advisory council or board, comprised of eminent scientists as well as public members who are interested in health issues or the biomedical sciences, determines the project's overall merit and priority in advancing the research agenda of the particular NIH funding institute. Altogether, about 38,500 research and training applications are reviewed annually through the NIH peer review system. At any given time, the NIH supports 35,000 grants in universities, medical schools, and other research and research training institutions both nationally and internationally.

The Intramural Research Programs, although representing only a small part of the total NIH budget, are central to the NIH scientific effort. First-rate scientists are key to NIH intramural research. They collaborate with one another regardless of institute affiliation or scientific discipline, and they have the intellectual freedom to pursue their research leads in the NIH's own laboratories. These explorations range from basic biology to behavioral research and studies on treatment of major diseases.

Scientific progress depends mainly on the scientist. About 50,000 principal investigators—working in every state and in several foreign countries, from every specialty in medicine, from every medical discipline, and at every major university and medical school—receive NIH extramural funding to explore unknown areas of medical science. Supporting and conducting the NIH's extramural and intramural programs are about 15,600 employees, more than 4,000 of whom hold professional or research doctorate degrees. The NIH staff includes intramural scientists, physicians, dentists, veterinarians, and nurses, and laboratory, administrative, and support personnel, plus an ever-changing array of research scientists in training.

The NIH has enabled scientists to learn much since its humble beginnings as a one-room laboratory in 1887. But many discoveries remain to be made. Among them are better ways to prevent and treat cancer, heart disease, stroke, blindness, arthritis, diabetes, kidney diseases, Alzheimer's disease, communication disorders, mental illness, drug abuse and alcoholism, AIDS and other unconquered diseases; ways to continue improving the health of infants and children, women, and minorities; and better ways to understand the aging process and behavior and lifestyle practices that affect health.

The Substance Abuse and Mental Health Services Administration (SAMHSA)

The Substance Abuse and Mental Health Services Administration was established by Congress under Public Law 102-321 on October 1, 1992. Its goal is to strengthen the capacity of the nation's health care delivery system to provide prevention, diagnosis, and treatment services for substance abusers and those with mental illnesses. SAMHSA builds on federal-state partnerships with communities and private organizations to address the needs of such individuals as well as to identify and respond to the community risk factors that contribute to these illnesses. In fiscal year 1999 SAMHSA's budget was approximately $2.5 billion. The agency employs approximately 550 staff members.

SAMHSA itself serves as the umbrella under which three centers are housed: the Center for Mental Health Services (CMHS), the Center for Substance Abuse Prevention (CSAP), and the Center for Substance Abuse Treatment (CSAT).

The Center for Mental Health Services and its programs are the legacy of decades of work to create an effective community-based mental health service infrastructure in the United States. The center's foremost goals are to improve the availability and accessibility of high-quality community-based services for people with or at risk for mental illnesses and their families. Although the largest portion of the center's annual appropriation supports states through the Community Mental Health Services Block Grant Program, the CMHS also supports a broadly based portfolio of grant programs designed to identify, test, and apply knowledge about the best community-based practices to reach the most at-risk people in our communities: adults with serious mental illnesses and children with serious emotional disturbances. Issues of stigma and consumer empowerment are also on the center's program and policy agenda. In addition, the center collects and disseminates national data on mental health services, designed to help inform future services policy and program decision making.

The Center for Substance Abuse Prevention serves as the national focal point for nationwide efforts to identify and promote effective strategies to prevent substance abuse—whether the abuse of illegal drugs, misuse of legal medications, use of tobacco, or excessive or illegal use of alcohol. As the sole federal agency with this charge, the CSAP's goal is to provide all Americans with the tools and knowledge they need to help reject substance abuse by strengthening families and communities and by developing knowledge of what interventions work best for which people. With grantees representing states, communities, and organizations at the national, regional, and local levels, the CSAP's grant activities support programs that promote the development, application, and dissemination of new knowledge in substance abuse prevention, whether focusing on preschool-age children and youth, or on older Americans. Further, the CSAP supports the National Clearinghouse for Alcohol and Drug Information (NCADI), the federal government's foremost source of information on substance abuse research, treatment, and prevention available for use by states, educational institutions, health care providers, and the public.

The Center for Substance Abuse Treatment provides national leadership in efforts to enhance the quality of substance abuse treatment services and ensure their availability to individuals who need them, including those with co-occurring drug, alcohol, mental, and physical problems. It works to identify, develop, and support policies and programs that enhance and expand science-based effective treatment services for individuals who abuse alcohol and other drugs and that address individuals' addiction-related problems. The CSAT administers the state block grant program for substance abuse prevention and treatment. While engaging with states to improve and enhance existing services under the block grant program, CSAT also undertakes significant knowledge development, education, and communications initiatives that identify and promote the best practices in the treatment of substance abusers and in intervention in finding resources when they need help.

Suggestions for
Further Reading

On HHS

Califano, Joseph A., Jr. *Governing America: An Insider's Report from the White House and the Cabinet.* New York: Simon and Schuster, 1981.

Kaufman, Herbert. *The Administrative Behavior of Federal Bureau Chiefs.* Washington, D.C.: Brookings Institution, 1981.

Miles, Rufus E., Jr. *The Department of H.E.W.* New York: Praeger, 1974.

Radin, Beryl A. "The Challenge of Managing Across Boundaries: The Case of the Office of the Secretary in the U.S. Department of Health and Human Services." Grant Report, PricewaterhouseCoopers Endowment for the Business of Government, November 2000.

————. "Managing Decentralized Departments: The Case of the U.S. Department of Health and Human Services." Grant Report, PricewaterhouseCoopers Endowment for the Business of Government, October 1999.

Shalala, Donna E. "Are Large Public Organizations Manageable?" *Public Administration Review* 58 (July–August 1998): 284–289.

Thompson, Penny R., and Mark R. Yessian. "Policy Analysis in the Office of Inspector General, U.S. Department of Health and Human Services." In *Organizations for Policy Analysis: Helping Government Think,* ed. Carol H. Weiss. Newbury Park, Calif.: Sage Publications, 1992.

Yessian, Mark. "The Generalist Perspective in the HEW Bureaucracy: An Account from the Field." *Public Administration Review* 40 (March–April 1980).

On Accountability and Related Issues

Aberbach, Joel D. *Keeping a Watchful Eye: The Politics of Congressional Oversight.* Washington, D.C.: Brookings Institution, 1990.

Aberbach, Joel D., and Bert A. Rockman. *In the Web of Politics, Three Decades of the U.S. Federal Executive.* Washington, D.C.: Brookings Institution Press, 2000.

Behn, Robert D. *Rethinking Democratic Accountability.* Washington, D.C.: Brookings Institution Press, 2001.

Burke, John. *Bureaucratic Responsibility.* Baltimore: Johns Hopkins University Press, 1986.

Doig, Jameson W., and Erwin C. Hargrove, eds. *Leadership and Innovation: Entrepreneurs in Government.* Baltimore: Johns Hopkins University Press, 1990.

Fesler, James W., and Donald F. Kettl. *The Politics of the Administrative Process.* 2d ed. Chatham, N.J.: Chatham House, 1996.

Gruber, Judith E. *Controlling Bureaucracies: Dilemmas in Democratic Governance.* Berkeley: University of California Press, 1987.

Heclo, Hugh. *A Government of Strangers: Executive Politics in Washington.* Washington, D.C.: Brookings Institution, 1977.

Kaufman, Herbert. *The Administrative Behavior of Federal Bureau Chiefs.* Washington, D.C.: Brookings Institution, 1981.

Kingdon, John W. *Agendas, Alternatives, and Public Policies.* 2d ed. New York: HarperCollins College Publishers, 1995.

Levin, Martin, and Mary Bryna Sanger. *Making Government Work: How Entrepreneurial Executives Turn Bright Ideas into Real Results.* San Francisco: Jossey Bass, 1994.

Light, Paul C. *Monitoring Government: Inspectors General and the Search for Accountability.* Washington, D.C.: Brookings Institution, 1993.

————. *Thickening Government: Federal Hierarchy and the Diffusion of Accountability.* Washington, D.C.: Brookings Institution, 1995.

Moore, Mark H. *Creating Public Value: Strategic Management in Government.* Cambridge: Harvard University Press, 1995.

Radin, Beryl A. *Beyond Machiavelli: Policy Analysis Comes of Age.* Washington, D.C.: Georgetown University Press, 2000.

Romzek, Barbara S., and Melvin J. Dubnick. "Accountability in the Public Sector: Lessons from the Challenger Tragedy." *Public Administration Review* 47 (May–June 1987): 227–238.

Rosen, Bernard. *Holding Government Bureaucracies Accountable.* 3d ed. Westport, Conn.: Praeger, 1998.

Rosenbloom, David H. *Building a Legislative-Centered Public Administration: Congress and the Administrative State, 1946–1999.* Tuscaloosa: University of Alabama Press, 2000.

Schick, Allen. *The Federal Budget: Politics, Policy, Process.* Rev. ed. Washington, D.C.: Brookings Institution, 2000.

Weber, Edward P. "The Question of Accountability in Historical Perspective." *Administration and Society* 31 (September 1999): 451–494.

Wilson, James Q. *Bureaucracy: What Government Agencies Do and Why They Do It.* New York: Basic Books, 1989.

Index